DRIVE IT!

The Complete Book of

HIGH SPEED DRIVING

on road & track

Peter Wherrett

Foulis

Haynes

A FOULIS Motoring Book

ISBN 0 85429 297 7
© **Peter Wherrett 1975**

This edition published 1981
First published under the title 'Motoring Skills & Tactics'
by Paul Hamlyn Pty. Ltd., Australia 1975

Published by
Haynes Publishing Group
Sparkford, Yeovil, Somerset BA22 7JJ, England

Distributed in North America by
Haynes Publications Inc
861 Lawrence Drive, Newbury Park,
California 91320 USA

Printed by Tien Wah Press (Pte) Limited
977 Bukit Timah Road, Singapore 21

Contents

ACKNOWLEDGMENTS
Our thanks are due to Brian McCarthy for his photographs, to *Racing Car News*, to Paul Gulson and to ABC-TV for their photographs.

Introduction

The talent of driving a car is a composite of three applications. The first, and perhaps the most important of these is attitude and, except to the extent that one is influenced by parents and peer groups, it is the only one of the three prerequisites that is unteachable. The second is knowledge. All knowledge is acquired by seeing, hearing and doing. In the case of driving a car it is preferable that as much knowledge be acquired as early as possible. The alternative is to drive without knowledge and this is obviously dangerous; the 'knowledge' acquired as a result of crashing a car into a pylon is of little benefit. The third application of driving is manipulative skill — the ability to handle the car with accuracy and confidence in any situation which might occur. This skill comes from a combination of attitude, knowledge and practice; to know is not necessarily to be able to do.

The fact that a driver acquires a book such as this and reads it indicates at least the beginnings of the right attitude. Reading and understanding will help to provide the knowledge, particularly when such learning is complimented by practical driving. Hence, also comes the skill. Such a book is not only for new drivers. Everyone can improve their driving and at a time in history when the private motor car is so wholly under question, morally, philosophically and economically, it behoves all of us drivers to lower costs and to reduce the number of automobile collisions.

Whether you are a new or old driver, good luck. You've never needed it more.

PETER WHERRETT

What's it all about?

1

WHAT'S IT ALL ABOUT?

You may drive a car for the first time at any age from about eight to eighty. If you do so at eight, it will probably be from on your father's knee and you will really only be steering. If you start at eighty you will be a very rare person indeed, for the saying about teaching old dogs new tricks is never truer than when applied to learning to drive a motor car. Whenever it is, wherever it is, the first time you drive, most of you will have a similar reaction. You will be both nervous and excited.

Nervous, because you are suddenly responsible for the mobility and control of a ton or more of steel and fabric and fuel and oil. Excited, because it is man's nature to be excited by such a challenge. If you are like most other people, you will very soon overcome both the nervousness and the excitement. Probably never again will you experience the pure thrill of your first drive. But if you are one of the few, or if with the help of this book, you can generate a real love of driving and of cars, you will repeat your first thrill almost every time you get behind the wheel—and certainly every time you are lucky enough to drive a new and exciting car or drive under new and exciting conditions.

For a while, when you begin to drive, you will be overawed by the array of instruments, switches, pedals and levers. You will probably be reasonably convinced that you will never learn what they are all for, let alone be able to synchronize their use to the point where it is all perfectly natural. But you will learn, and you should learn properly.

When you drive for the first time there are other people interested in your progress as well. People you don't even know and, in all probability, never will. There are the authorities who will test you for and issue your driving licence, the police, the traffic authorities, the politicians and road builders and car salesmen and more. But most of all, there is your fellow motorist who is also probably not yet a *driver*. Your fellow motorist is already out there going places, sitting in traffic queues, suffering breakdowns and flat tyres and having collisions. If you are like the great majority of other motorists you will believe that it can never happen to you—the inevitable collision, that is. Famous last thoughts!

Your attitude to your fellow motorist is as significant to your driving as your attitude to your own family and your own car. He must be treated with care and consideration. You must be tolerant with him, you must share with him and you must accept that he has as much right to be on the road as you have. He may or may not be as good a motorist as you—if he is not, you should have sympathy for him and help him through the difficulties in which he will involve himself. If it is obvious that he is as good as you, you should not try to dispute the point nor try to prove that you are better. The only people who try to prove how good they are behind the wheel are those who are unsure of their skills. When you know you are good there is no further need to prove it to anyone—unless you are racing, and then it becomes a different matter altogether. More of that later.

But why should you be a good driver? Why, when it is obvious that most other drivers have reached only mediocre standards, should you make every honest effort to be a skilled motorist? In the most candid terms I can express, you are obligated to do so—obligated to all those other people, and also to yourself. In any task, one's own self respect requires that one do the task as well as possible. More so when people's lives are at stake, as they definitely are in motoring. To play your part in stemming the mounting death toll, you must learn to drive with skill, confidence and initiative. You must also learn to drive within the limitations provided by the highways systems, the car manufacturers and the law.

For many years a great number of people have been campaigning for better driver education. I'm with them—but I invariably go further. Most of the campaigners are referring to basic tuition—the use of controls, traffic sense, an intelligent understanding of the laws of the road. There is so much more. In a discussion on the subject of driver education with someone who should have known better (he was a member of an advanced driving institute), I once insisted that the complete motorist should know how to get out of a vicious and unpredictable oversteer slide. My protagonist, firstly, did not know what an oversteer slide was and, secondly, when I had explained it to him, was adamant that a good driver should not ever get into such a situation. Later, when I describe in some detail what an oversteer slide is, you will understand what I mean when I say that to avoid a slide of this type even occasionally, you would have to drive all the time at less than 40 mph. And if you do so, you are not a complete driver.

The complete driver can confidently keep up with the traffic flow. On the open highway he can drive at the speed limit with assurance and accuracy. Thus he does not present the hazard we so often strike of a motorist pottering along 25 mph under the limit and making himself into a mobile chicane. Now you might say that there is no law which says that you have to drive up to the speed limit. There certainly is. It is the law of common sense and good manners. When it is safe for the bulk of the surrounding traffic to motor at 60 mph and when they are obviously doing so, you must keep pace with them. Interrupting the natural traffic flow is a major cause of collisions on the open road.

We have to live with the motor car and we therefore have to live with the motorist. The car, whether we like it or not, is a significant and important part of our lives and it seems highly unlikely that it will decrease in importance in the next twenty years.

In the United States of America, where there are more motor cars than in any other country on earth, they have a major traffic problem already. And this, despite the most elaborate highways and main roads system of all.

Since the invention of the wheel back in the third millenium B.C. (which is some time ago), man has become increasingly dependent on his world on wheels—and increasingly alarmed at the end result of such dependence. The toll in human life alone is incredible; for instance, in the last thirty years, more than one million people have died on American roads alone. What is it in man's nature that will make him spend hundreds of dollars having his children taught a competitive sport and then skimp as far as possible to get them a driving licence in the shortest possible time? What is it that causes the same man to spend weeks in the air learning to fly and barely hours on the ground learning how to drive? Specially when flying is obviously less dangerous!

Another pupil once said to me following his advanced training, 'That's the best £20 I ever spent'. When I asked him, 'Why?' he said that he had not had so much fun in years. I asked him if he thought he had learned something as well, and he remarked, 'Oh! Good heavens, yes. But I wouldn't have thought the money was well spent to learn something about driving—unless I thought it could be fun as well.'

And that's about it. Sport is fun. It's worth money. Flying is fun. It's worth money. Driving is a chore, a means of getting from place to place, only. It is not worth money. At least, it's not until it gets to be fun—and then you will change your family hack for a sporty car which will cost you twice as much. You may even enter a competitive motoring event or two and happily pay the usually large entry fee. You will buy expensive driving gloves, new accessories which will add to your car's safety and performance.

Now driving is fun and you will love every minute of it. Join the Club!

Basics

2

BASICS

It will be completely obvious the moment I say it, but I'll say it anyway. The primary requirement for any driver is that he be in complete control of his car at all times. But, having said that, I'd now like to elaborate upon it. The question we might ask at this point is, 'When is a car out of control?' A car is out of control when it is doing what it wants to do rather than what its driver wants it to do. Significantly, however, this point varies from driver to driver. By way of example, a skilled racing driver may still be exercising some form of control over his car even as it progressively demolishes itself along a safety fence. A nervous unskilled road driver, however, may have lost control the minute a car appears unexpectedly from a side street. Which seems to indicate that the driver might have lost control of himself rather than the car. Perhaps therefore we need to look more closely at 'control', in its various forms.

There are three progressive stages of control. *Defensive control* is the form of control a driver normally exercises in his day-to-day driving. That is, the form of control which allows the driver to avoid potentially dangerous situations. It requires complete concentration, a certain amount of basic skill, common sense and a working knowledge of the laws of the road. It is defensive control which keeps most of us from having some form of collision every time we drive. But it is both idealistic and unrealistic to believe that defensive control will always work. No one is that perfect. The most law-abiding, safety-conscious driver is still capable of making a mistake. An error of judgment of speed, distance or radius of a curve, a miscalculation of time, a brief moment of inattention, and the second control system will have to come into effect for the driver to avoid a collision.

Reaction control is a twofold system. It allows for the reaction of both the driver and the car. When a driver's defensive control system breaks down something happens which provokes a reaction from him. For example, an alert, keen driver on a straight road takes his eyes off the road for just a fraction of a second. The road is lined with trees and, even while he was paying attention, he did not notice the narrow entranceway to a farm ahead on his left. As he switches his attention back to the road ahead he is immediately aware that a careless driver is bringing his truck out from the side lane on to the road without having checked the traffic flow first. Our driver's instinctive reaction is one of fright and no matter how brief the fright moment is it will have been sufficient for him to have taken his foot off the accelerator and jumped on the brake. I say 'jumped' because he will have done exactly that. The instinctive fright reaction is to momentarily panic. As soon as he hits the pedal, there is a violent reaction from the car and it may begin to slew sideways. The reasons for its doing so are not important at this point but they could be numerous. What happens from here on will depend entirely upon the driver's ability to effect reaction control. First he must control his own reaction. He cannot avoid the 'fright', because it is human nature to register shock in such a situation, but he can control it. However, he can only control the reaction if experience and training tell him what to do next.

Let's say that the experience and training are missing in this case. Inevitably the driver will 'freeze' in the brakes locked situation he has provoked because there

Common Sense: It is common sense not to take a dangerous right of way just because it's legally allowed

are no further messages coming from the brain to tell him what to do next. He knows the car is slewing sideways and he recognizes that it is going out of control but he has no knowledge or prior experience to draw from to correct the situation. He may or may not hit the offending truck; he may or may not spin across the road into the oncoming traffic; he may or may not spin off the side of the road into a ditch or a conveniently located tree or power pole. But whatever happens is entirely in the hands of providence. The driver is simply sitting at the wheel waiting for the inevitable.

Now let's look at a really skilled driver. In the same situation he will also react in fright because it is human nature to do so. He will see the truck and instinctively hit the brakes hard. But this time as the car begins to slew sideways there will be both knowledge and experience to draw from. He will quickly turn the front wheels to make sure they are continuing to point in the direction of intended travel and slightly release the brake pedal pressure to allow the wheels to unlock and roll again. As they do so, the car will kick straight again and he will straighten the steering wheel accordingly. Thereafter he will squeeze the brake pedal less violently, trying to avoid a second lock up.

His reaction control has been effective in that he is still driving the car and in command of the situation. But it may be that the dramatic moment is not over yet. Let's say that the distance from our driver's car to the truck is too short for the driver to be able to stop in time. If the driver lacked further training and experience he would go on pushing the brake pedal until the wheels locked again. At the slower speed and with less violent use of the pedal, it's probable that the car will not again slew sideways, but once the front wheels are locked the driver is no longer able to steer the car. The locked front wheels are sliding on the road surface and the loss of adhesion precludes them from responding to the steering. Ultimately, the driver is going to crash into the truck. If it was not an emergency earlier, it certainly is now and the driver should have exercised some form of 'last ditch' *emergency control.*

Back to the skilled driver then. Having regained control of the car, he soon realizes that he has not the distance to stop in time. He also knows that if he locks the wheels he will not be able to steer. That knowledge alone makes it possible for the driver to control the car. It may still crash—even such skills are no guarantee that you will always avoid a collision. But obviously they help.

The point is clear then. Our skilled, experienced driver was still in control of the situation even at the point of impact. He had used two forms of control in addition to the defensive control system he would use in all his driving.

However, utilizing the reaction and emergency control systems proficiently requires practice and knowledge. So before they confound you completely, read the rest of the book, then come back and read this section again.

We shall now explore the other basic requirements of a skilled driver and couple them all to the defensive control system. These basic requirements are:

1. common sense
2. observation
3. concentration
4. judgement
5. anticipation
6. courtesy.

All of these go hand in hand. If you are lacking even one of them, you will never be a skilful driver. Obviously, the most important of them is *common sense.* Without common sense, any other acquired driving techniques are wasted. To breach the rules of common sense is to blatantly breach the most significant of the traffic regulations. If you have no common sense you will not qualify as a safe and competent road user. You know what it is and you know what it means so there is no need to dwell on it.

15

Observation: The feet under the truck should tell you something

Concentration: Avoid having your attention distracted at any time while you are driving

Being *observant* is the second of our six basics and again it is far too little practised. Being observant means so much more than just being aware of the traffic around you. You must watch everything that may have some bearing on your driving. You must watch the road ahead, both well ahead and immediately in front of you, side streets, parked cars, children playing, pedestrians, cyclists and your rear vision mirror or mirrors all in an instant. On the open road, you must watch for animals, broken road shoulders, a change in the road surface, patches of water, branches of trees, the traffic and any direction from which it might come, particularly from behind. If you are in a line of traffic, watch the car at least three in front of you. This will make you more responsive to the car immediately in front. By being observant you will be able to anticipate and this is half the battle in being able to take corrective or avoiding action.

You will have to agree that you cannot be observant unless you are prepared to *concentrate*. Lapses in concentration, at any speed, very often prove fatal. The job in hand when you are driving is of such magnitude that at times you should be concentrating as hard as you would on a game of squash or tennis or any of your favourite sports. There will be times when you should avoid conversation and turn off your car radio. In fact, if you are easily distracted you should not talk or have your radio on at any time. Leave all that for when you stop.

Judgement: Be aware of radius of curve, speed of entry, and correct line

Anticipation: Assume there may be an unseen danger over every crest

Judgement is something you usually either have or do not have. But, to some extent, it can be developed with practice. There are three things you have to be able to judge accurately, if you are to be a good driver. They are *speed, distance* and *radius of a curve.* If for any reason at all you have found that your judgement is not good, you should certainly never drive fast and, to compensate, you should concentrate harder. You can develop your judgement by estimating speeds and distances and checking your guess against your odometer and speedometer. Try it when you are on the beach or in a park—guess the distance to a certain point and then pace it out to see how close you were. To practise estimating speed, get hold of a stop-watch, tape your speedometer over and try to drive at a fixed speed over a pre-measured distance. Do not, however, do this on public roads in heavy traffic. Find a quiet country road or a section of private road. In these ways you can improve your judgement and this, in turn, will improve your driving.

Being able to *anticipate* the actions of other road users and, for that matter, pedestrians, is obviously another significant point. As we have already seen, anticipation follows observation. It sometimes almost requires a sixth sense to guess what some drivers are about to do. Everyone has had the experience of seeing a driver make a sudden turn with no warning or stop for no apparent reason. These people make anticipation very difficult but, if you watch closely, most drivers will give some warning of their intentions. A sudden look around or a shift in driving position, a flick of brake lights while he makes up his mind; any of these points should give you cause to anticipate some action and will prepare you for counter-action on your part. Anticipation will help keep you out of trouble. It will make you more responsive and a safer driver. It is a technique which must not be regarded too lightly.

Courtesy: When it makes no difference to your progress anyway, it is helpful to let the other driver into the line of traffic

You should be able to achieve 180 degrees of turn without moving the hands and without becoming cramped or strained

The last of the basic requirements is *courtesy*—but it is far from being the least important. Courtesy comes usually with a pleasant disposition but people who are easily put out need to exercise self-control. Giving another driver his legal right is not only necessary but also gratifying, particularly if he gives you a wave of acknowledgement in return. There is no point in trying to get even with someone who causes you a bad moment on the road. Let him have his way and control your urge to get even; this will result in a feeling of satisfaction at your own tolerance of people who perhaps do not drive as well as you. When someone wants to overtake you, let him, no matter what the circumstances. If you think he is going to be in trouble with an oncoming car, try to make room for him to get in front of you. You know he was foolish to try it. There is no reason for you to bring yourself down to his level by keeping him out where he will be in real trouble. Your superior judgement and anticipation will enable you to decide for him whether he can make it or not and, although he will not show any gratitude, you have your satisfaction in knowing that your skill helped to avoid a dangerous situation.

If you can master all the basics you are well on the way to being a good driver. But there is still much to learn and many points you must be aware of. While we are still dealing with basics, however, it might be as well to mention the occasions when you should never drive.

No one is capable of driving a car in a safe and competent manner when he is *tired*, when he is *angry* or when he has been *drinking*. When he is tired he is likely to go to sleep at the wheel but, even if he does not, he will certainly fall short on a number of the basics. He will not be able to concentrate and his judgement will be impaired. If he becomes tired on a long trip he should stop and refresh himself either by taking a short sleep or by having a meal and a rest. A driver who is angry is also inefficient, unless he possesses great self-control. Anger clouds common sense, concentration and judgement. A person in a temper is a potentially dangerous driver. He will almost certainly be also lacking courtesy. Drinking and driving has been the subject of so much publicity that it hardly seems necessary to mention it here. Suffice to say that excessive alcohol will rob a driver of most, or even all, of the basic skills. Your attitude to driving under these conditions is entirely a personal one in that you must live with your own conscience. You alone know your tolerance to alcohol. It is against the law to drink and drive and the breathalyser allows no margin for error. No more need be said.

Apart from the mental attitudes and skills we have so far discussed there are many points regarding a driver's physical requirements that we now need to consider. 'Physical' here includes the driver himself, his car and his equipment. First, from the driver's personal point of view, there is the simple matter of physical fitness to be considered. This applies not only to major disabilities but also to minor bruises and strains which can restrict sudden movement, particularly of arms and legs. A strained thigh muscle can make lifting your leg from accelerator to brake a painful operation which it is difficult to do quickly in an emergency. The same applies to a shoulder or arm where a sudden turn of the wheel may be hampered by your automatic reaction to pain; this will increase your reaction time. The point here is that, if you have such an injury, you should test yourself at the wheel of a stationary car before driving it. If you are restricted in any way which would make driving even slightly more dangerous than usual, don't drive until your injury or disability is healed.

Reach to controls. In this case the shift lever is too far away to reach without stretching

Good instrumentation, easily readable, shrouded from glare

The second point to be considered is equally important and equally ignored by many drivers. It takes the form of a simple question: Does the car fit you? The question is put in this way because obviously it is easy enough to change the car, but it is impossible to change the shape of the driver. It is vital that a driver be relaxed at the wheel of his car. This assists in warding off fatigue and ensures that the mind is free to concentrate on the task of driving. A driver should be able to adopt the correct driving position and

1. comfortably reach the brake, clutch and accelerator pedals without moving in his seat,
2. handle the steering wheel through 180 degrees of turn each way without becoming restrained and cramped,
3. reach the gear shift through all extremities of operation without having to stretch,
4. read all instruments in as brief as possible a moment by eye movement only,
5. reach the emergency brake (hand) with his seat belt done up and properly adjusted.

If a car fails on any one of the above, even more care should be taken in driving it and open road driving speeds should be reduced accordingly. If it fails on all, it does not fit and it should be replaced as soon as practicable by something that does.

Thirdly, a good driver should have certain personal equipment, particularly for use on longer trips. He should have either a pair of good quality driving gloves which will absorb moisture from the hands and prevent them from becoming slippery on the steering wheel or the wheel should be covered with a leather or vinyl binding or glove. If a steering wheel cover is fitted it should be very tight so that it will not slip on the wheel. The driver should wear comfortable and loose-fitting clothes and should preferably drive without coat and tie. He should wear shoes of light leather with a heel grip and thin soles. If he is worried by glare he should have at his fingertips a pair of good quality sunglasses. His car should have a lap-and-diagonal or full harness seat belt, correctly fitted and adjusted so that it is firm without being uncomfortable. The buckle should be at the driver's hip with a lap-and-diagonal belt and in the soft portion of the stomach if a full harness is fitted.

All of this equipment should be in constant use, although in some cases the use of special driving shoes may be impractical. Seat belts should always be used—for reasons which have been made very obvious over the past years.

After a driver has checked his car for fit, there are a number of other points to be checked. These points will apply in varying degrees depending on whether you own the car, have borrowed it or perhaps have it on hire. If the car is yours, your regular routine inspections and checks should include what we are about to consider. If it is borrowed or hired you should check certain things before you drive it on a trip and particularly if you intend to drive faster than about 50 mph.

You should at all times be aware of the condition of your tyres. Are they getting low on tread? Are they retreads? Are they cross ply or radial? What is the manufacturer's recommended maximum safe speed? Are there stone fractures or wall cracks? Are the pressures right? Your lights should be checked and any broken bulbs replaced immediately. Exhaust systems should be checked for leaks. Brakes should be checked as a matter of routine every time you get into the car. Where possible check the wheels for cracks, particularly around the wheel nut holes. Make sure that the wheel nuts are tight and that they are bedding on metal, not paint. If there is paint under a wheel nut, remove the nut and scrape the paint away. Wheel nuts are inclined to loosen if they have a coat of paint between them and the wheel. Are all the windows clean?

Here is a recommended check list which you should carry out on the occasions specified.

DAILY

brakes	full pedal, hand brake holding
lights	all working including stop and turn lights
windows	clear all round
seat belts	properly adjusted before you move

WEEKLY (or before each long trip) daily check as above, plus

tyres	tread depth, cracks, fractures, pressures
wiper blades	perished, tension gone

MONTHLY all above plus

steering	for wear and breakage
brake hoses	for wear or rubbing or fouling
suspension	spring and shock mountings for wear or breakage

At this stage we have discussed the basic requirements for driving a car. Let's recapitulate. We have agreed on six basics so far as mental attitudes are concerned. They were common sense, observation, concentration, judgement, anticipation and courtesy. We have also agreed that a driver must be physically fit and that he must be properly equipped. His car must also be properly equipped and must fit him, and he must regularly carry out certain checks to ensure that it is safe to drive.

Special Basics

3

SPECIAL BASICS

1. Exaggerated stiff-arm position—the driver is too far back for satisfactory reach and not sufficiently relaxed

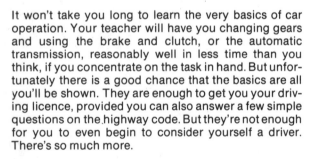

The lap-and-diagonal seat belt should cross the chest without rubbing against the neck or collar and the buckle should be located on or about the hip. Note that the driver is not wearing either coat or tie, but is wearing sun glasses, all in the interests of maximum comfort and efficiency

2. The driver is too close to achieve maximum efficient control. Movements are cramped and the body is tense

It won't take you long to learn the very basics of car operation. Your teacher will have you changing gears and using the brake and clutch, or the automatic transmission, reasonably well in less time than you think, if you concentrate on the task in hand. But unfortunately there is a good chance that the basics are all you'll be shown. They are enough to get you your driving licence, provided you can also answer a few simple questions on the highway code. But they're not enough for you to even begin to consider yourself a driver. There's so much more.

SITTING AT THE WHEEL

When you climb in behind the steering wheel of any car, well before you move off into the traffic stream, you should make sure that you are comfortable; that you can reach all controls and switches; and that your seat belt is adjusted properly. Put your hands on the wheel and check the positioning of the upper part of your body. If your arms are bent and your elbows close to your chest, you are too close to the wheel and will not be able to apply much turn in either direction without finding your movements restricted. If. on the other hand, your arms are outstretched, reaching for the

3. The correct position provides comfort, reach and maximum freedom of movement

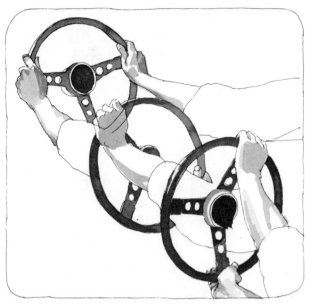

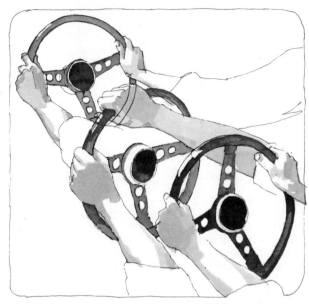

1. *Where possible avoid re-locating the hands on the steering wheel. Simply turn into the corner and centralize on the exit*

2. *The alternative method requires constant repositioning of the hands as the wheel is fed through in the 'push-pull' system*

wheel, you are too far away. You will find it difficult to apply sufficient turn without moving your hands and you will tire quickly. Move the seat on its runners until you can sit with your hands in the 'quarter to three' position and with your elbows just bent. Turn left as much as you can. If you can cross your arms so that the elbows almost touch, and then do the same when you turn right, you are in the ideal seating position. But, before you set the seat, check to make sure that you can still get full travel on the clutch and brake without stretching your legs. Some cars are built so badly that when your arms are set properly you can't operate the pedals. If this is so with the car you are about to drive, you will have to compensate a little to achieve a seating position which will provide the nearest to the ideal and still allow accurate operation of all controls. Then set the seat and/or squab.

My second reason for advocating the 'fixed hand' method is connected with slide control; we will cover this in more detail later. Suffice at this stage to say that when a car slides on the rear wheels the driver must act quickly and accurately to correct the slide. It is necessary to straighten the steering wheel to at least the straight ahead position and then perhaps even put on some turn in the opposite direction. With his hands in a constant position on the wheel, first, the driver can tell exactly when his front wheels are pointing straight ahead, and second, he can bring the steering wheel back to this position and apply corrective turns so much faster. It is far easier to prove the point in practice that it is in theory but the diagrams will give a better idea of the method.

Once a driver has mastered the constant hand position for all his normal driving, and particularly for the open road, I have no argument against his adopting the 'push pull' method for city or slow driving. But I am convinced that for the average driver the 'push pull' method cannot work in situations of difficulty or panic.

THE STEERING WHEEL
I have just said that you should place your hands on the steering wheel in the 'quarter to three' position. From this position you can apply the greatest amount of leverage and turn the wheel without having to re-locate your hands on the wheel. Although this is the ideal position, it is reasonable to compromise to 'ten to two' if this is more comfortable in your car.

From this point onwards we run into differences of opinion as to how the wheel should be turned. Many people advocate the 'push pull' or 'shuffle' method of steering. In this method the hands are kept almost constantly in the 'quarter to three' or 'ten to two' position and the wheel is fed through by pushing up and pulling down with the opposite hands. Having rounded the corner or curve the wheel is re-set to straight ahead by the same method. I disagree with the 'push pull' method for two quite clear-cut reasons.

The first is that it is un-natural for most people. It is a steering technique that has to be taught. My eight-year-old son indicated quite clearly to me when he first drove a 'go-kart' that, with no instruction at all, most people will turn the steering wheel with their hands in a fixed position on the wheel. This has been substantiated by observing people on our advanced driving courses: the great majority begin their turn without re-locating their hands on the wheel.

It is possible to turn the steering wheel through nearly 180 degrees before you have to move either hand, and 180 degrees of turn will put you through most open road curves. For city driving the method of turning for slower, tighter corners becomes the 'hand over hand' method. Again, this is the method used by most people and it is the most natural. When it is impractical to try to turn further without moving the hands, first one hand and then the other takes a new grip on the wheel to complete the turn. The wheel is returned to the straight ahead position by the same method.

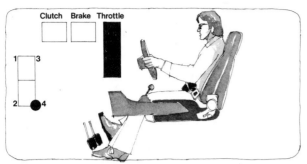

1. We are changing from fourth gear to third gear in an H-pattern manual shift car

2. Clutch disengaged—shift to neutral

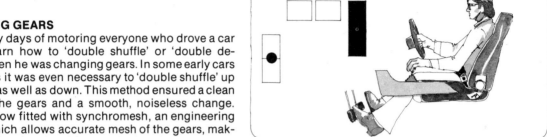

3. Clutch engaged—rev the engine

4. Clutch disengaged—complete shift to third

5. Shift completed, accelerate or decelerate as appropriate

CHANGING GEARS

In the early days of motoring everyone who drove a car had to learn how to 'double shuffle' or 'double declutch' when he was changing gears. In some early cars and trucks it was even necessary to 'double shuffle' up the gears as well as down. This method ensured a clean mesh of the gears and a smooth, noiseless change. Cars are now fitted with synchromesh, an engineering feature which allows accurate mesh of the gears, making it easier for the driver to make clean accurate changes.

Synchromesh on manual cars and, of course, the automatic gearbox, have largely taken the challenge out of driving. Despite this, the good driver—the driver who wants to get better and the sporting driver—still use the 'double shuffle' technique, specially for down shifting. When a driver changes gear he is matching the engine speed (measured in revolutions per minute—rpm) and the speed of the transmission to his required road speed. As everyone knows, a car's engine will rev very hard in first gear if the driver tries to drive too fast in that gear. By changing up to the next (higher) gear he gains road speed and reduces engine revs. As the change is made, the driver takes his foot *off* the accelerator. The engine revs drop and the higher gear is selected. When the clutch is engaged again the lower engine speed approximately matches the new road speed.

In changing down the situation, naturally enough, is exactly the opposite. The driver who is in fourth gear and who wants third gear should bring the engine speed up as he engages the lower gear. With synchromesh he is able to simply push the change through and then engage the clutch again, with the result that, for a brief moment as the transmission forces the engine up in revs, the transmission will be under a considerable load. Possibly the rear wheels will even lock up for a moment while the engine adjusts.

The 'double shuffle' change is the method by which the driver brings the engine revs up manually so that the change down is smoother and places less load on the transmission. This is how it's done. The driver makes the usual movements as far as neutral gear. That is, he disengages the clutch and shifts the lever to the neutral position. Then he engages the clutch briefly and, with it engaged, hits the accelerator pedal bringing the engine revs up to or slightly beyond those required for the lower year. Quickly then, he disengages the clutch and completes the change. He has matched the engine revolutions to the road speed and in so doing has avoided the possibility of rear wheel lock up and also lessened the strain on the gearbox and back axle assembly. The down change is much smoother, the balance and stability of the car is maintained and the costly wear factor is reduced. The advantages of such a method of gear change become obvious.

In cars with synchromesh it is true that the mid-way clutch engagement is not entirely necessary. It is desirable though, because it takes the strain from the synchromesh mechanism and ensures its longer life. In fact, the shift lever can be passed straight through, and while this is being done the accelerator is depressed to bring up the engine revs.

For a while you may find it difficult to judge how many revs you need to synchronize the change perfectly. Remember, better too many than too few. By way of example think about this. In 4th gear at 40 mph the engine is revolving at, say, 2,500 rpm. The difference between 4th gear and 3rd gear is, again say, 1,000 rpm. So at 40 mph, to engage 3rd gear you will need 3,500 rpm. It's easy if you have a tachometer in your car because then you can read off the engine revs as you make the change. But in most cars you will have to play it by ear, literally. Try it; see how much smoother you can be.

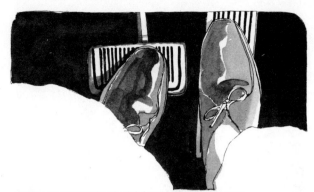

The location of the feet for left foot braking in automatics

AUTOMATICS

For years the standard recommendation for anyone driving an automatic car has been to put away your left foot. In the early days this suggestion may have been justifiable because most drivers were adapting from manual to automatic cars and there was a tendency for the left foot to instinctively react as a clutch foot and stab at the brake pedal in an emergency—with dire results.

However, the left foot can play a very significant part in driving automatic cars. And while its use is relatively easy for a new driver (who is not accustomed to using the left foot for clutch operation), it is also not difficult for a regular manual transmission driver to change over to left foot braking in an automatic, if he is prepared to concentrate on using the method I'm going to describe. But first, let's consider left foot braking in automatics.

It has always seemed ridiculous to me that one should use one foot for two pedals and have another foot sitting back doing nothing. Purely from a commonsense point of view two pedals can be much better operated by two feet. Let me say, also, right now, that in some countries a new driver who learns left foot braking and uses this system when taking a licence test just might be failed for it. Which just goes to prove how far behind the times our accepted systems of motoring can be.

Think about it for a minute. You are driving along in normal metropolitan traffic with your left foot idly lying back and your right foot constantly jumping from accelerator to brake and back again. In heavy traffic if your left foot were poised above or resting gently on the brake pedal, it would simply be a matter of left foot to *slow,* right foot to *go.* Such operation gives you the opportunity to better anticipate potential danger. Coming to a concealed intersection, you just ease off the accelerator with the right foot and at the same time lift the left foot into position above the brake. Should there be a problem, the left foot simply goes to work. Importantly, this saves the fraction of a second of time (and consequently distance), involved in bringing the right foot across. In effect, it means a shorter stopping dis-

tance and also better overall control because the transition from *go* to *slow* to *go* is smoother.

If you are a new driver there is no reason why you should not begin by learning left foot braking right from the start. If you would like to convert, the best way is to do it in stages. Divide the braking function into two types: planned and unplanned braking. Planned braking is all the braking you do that you think about first—in heavy traffic, approaching intersections, corners or curves for example. Unplanned braking is the unexpected braking you have to do from time to time. At its ultimate extent this is emergency situation braking. Practise using the left foot for all planned braking. In this way you can consciously develop the same degree of feel and sensitivity in your left foot that you have developed over the years in your right foot. At this stage don't try to use the left foot for unplanned braking. For some time your right foot will move to the brake pedal instinctively when a potential crisis arises. Eventually you will find that your conscious left foot braking will condition you to using the same foot for unplanned braking and you ultimately will be using your left foot all the time.

Many people have already discovered how effective the left foot can be in tight manoeuvring situations. Parking and slow reversing for example are ideal opportunities to develop left foot braking and you will quickly find how much additional control you will have. Once you have mastered the technique you will find that it can also give a great deal of added control for open road cornering. The technique is simple enough. You approach the curve and lift the left foot into position on the brake. Squeeze gently to reduce your corner entry speed and go on lightly braking into the early part of the turn. Then ease the power on with the right foot while the left foot is still effecting some brake control. There is a slight overlap of operations. As you wish to increase power, ease the left foot off the brake. In this way there is no period where the car is not being controlled by one operation or the other and its balance and stability will be greatly enhanced.

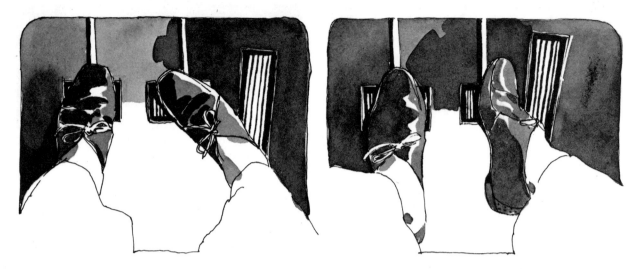

The alternatives for 'heel and toe' down shifting. Only the method shown on the left actually uses the heel and the toe. The other, for reasons of pedal location, simply utilizes the ball of the foot and the side of the foot

One final word of warning about left foot braking. There is a tendency, particularly while you are learning, to ride the brake pedal much as you may have done at one time with the clutch. Beware! You will overheat the brakes and you will be wearing out pad and lining material much faster.

HEEL AND TOE

The last of the special basic techniques you should acquire to become the complete driver is that known as 'heel and toe'. It applies only to manually geared cars, and in fact, is badly named for today's cars. Both name and technique originated in motor racing in the mid-thirties where the 'double shuffle' down shift was essential since the gear boxes of the day had no synchromesh. The process of matching engine revs to gear and road speed was part and parcel of the corner approach procedure and drivers found it impossible to brake, declutch, and hit the throttle for engine revs at the same moment. So the car designers found a way to locate the throttle pedal in such position that the driver could operate both throttle and brake with the same (the right) foot. Literally, the ball of the foot (or toes) goes on the brake and the heel on the throttle—hence 'heel and toe'. Modern car designers very rarely think about such techniques when they build today's cars but it is, nevertheless, possible to use such a technique in most cars in one way or another.

It becomes a very useful system of car control for those who recognize and exploit the rev matching down shifting procedure. Imagine it: let's say you are out on a country road, a twisty one. You are approaching a fairly tight corner from a straight and you can see that you will need a lower gear for that corner than the one you are currently using. Your road speed dictates that you must brake before you shift as your speed would be too high for the lower gear. So, you gently brake with the ball of your foot and begin to reduce speed. At the same time you are evaluating the radius and shape of the curve and you decide on third gear. If you stopped braking now for a moment while you moved your foot back to the accelerator to bring up the engine revs for your change you would also stop

slowing down and your corner approach speed may well still be too high.

You continue to brake and you roll the side of your foot or your heel (depending on the pedal arrangement) on to the throttle and carry out the down change. Because you are not on and off the brake and because you have been able to match engine revs to gears to road speed, the whole change is much smoother and you have a more stable car at the point of entry into the corner. The technique is not easy because it requires even more effective co-ordination than normal changes need but, like anything worth doing, it will come if you practise.

There are those who suggest that 'heel and toe' is only effective for racing, but I entirely disagree. I have known of people who have exploited the technique to effectively get themselves out of what might otherwise have been a difficult situation. In fact, once it is acquired you can use it just as effectively in metropolitan driving. Approach a left turn at intersection—brake gently—roll up engine revs just before turn point—engage clutch smoothly—accelerate through. The least you can do is give it a try.

Road Sense
and Sensitivity

4

ROAD SENSE AND SENSITIVITY

Interestingly, in Australia, a few years ago a number of road safety organizations in their campaigns for safety on the roads came up with the slogan 'Courtesy is Catching'. They exploited it for some considerable time but, as with most well-founded campaigns, the 'courtesy' campaign fell on deaf ears. Courtesy was not, and in fact is not, catching. Partly the problem lies in the nature of the average driver. When he is at the wheel of a car the male of the species in particular is generally unable to concede that he may be wrong, and certainly determined to bring every minor skirmish on the roads to a potentially violent head. Many times you see such situations. Someone, through ignorance or thoughtlessness, has failed to give right of way at an intersection. The wronged driver, instead of compensating for the other driver's mistake, has made things worse by driving as close as he can to the other car, blowing his horn, shouting abuse at the top of his voice and generally making the situation potentially even more dangerous. Even though they may miss each other on this occasion, both drivers leave the scene as 'uptight' as they could be; both are now preoccupied with the 'near miss' and well on the way to scoring a 'direct hit' within the next mile or so.

All this brings me to the point of attitude. While I consider that skill can compensate to some extent for a wrong attitude on the road, I still believe that a little more forgiveness, tolerance and understanding on the part of drivers would reduce the collision rate remarkably.

On the relationship between skill and attitude, let's consider a prime example. The youthful 'hot-rodder' with quick young reflexes and sharp eyes and ears is potentially the best driver on our roads. He is also, in this case, fully trained and appreciative of the equipment he commands. But he is desperate to show everyone how good he is. He has no regard for other road users and is far too aggressive in his driving habits. His attitude will get him into some sort of trouble almost every time he drives—his skill might get him out of it again.

Take a similar driver, equally a self-designated 'hot-shoe', with the same attitude and the same aggression. But untrained. Unable to control the car in a really tight situation, only because he has llttle or no natural skill and no one has ever taught him properly. His attitude will also get him into trouble. For a while, luck and his quick reflexes will save him from disaster. But it will happen eventually. With his car overloaded with enthusiastic friends, possibly even with a skinful of his favourite alcoholic drink, he will put the car in a situation which requires pure skill to pull it out again. The pure skill that just does not exist. Headlines!

It's so much easier to work on skill than it is on attitude. Only maturity and wisdom will modify attitude. Everyone can be taught the skills, at least to some extent. These two qualities, attitude and skill, I refer to as 'road sense' and 'sensitivity'. Let's elaborate somewhat on each.

ROAD SENSE

It is obvious when the subject of road sense is introduced, to immediately think of the hooligan type driver and to relate road sense as an attitude which he, as a classic example, does not possess. While this is entirely true in many cases, it would be erroneous to overlook the quiet, apparently safe motorist, who in a great many cases is also sadly lacking in road sense. Road sense I define as the ability to live with the situations, conditions, and hazards which occur in your everyday motoring; to accept them and to be unobtrusive, inoffensive and unobstructive in your control of them.

In a line of heavy traffic just keeping up with the car immediately in front is road sense. Dawdling along, unconcerned about the welfare of other drivers, presenting a continuing hazard, is nearly as bad a practice as trying to pass them all.

To arrive at an intersection in a situation where you have legal right of way and enforce that right of way regardless of the possible consequences is dangerous and unnecessary, and indicates an equal lack of road sense. This particularly applies where the car that should give way to you has no other car for some distance behind it. As you have slowed for the intersection anyway, it is easier and safer for you to allow the other car to continue its unhindered progress and move out after it has passed than it would be for you to push out in front, despite the fact that you technically have right of way. That's road sense.

To drive in the centre lane of a dual-carriageway when the left-hand lane is clear is a good example of a lack of road sense. Even though you may be driving at, or above, the speed limit for the road, there is no justification for you playing traffic controller in an effort to make sure everyone else stays behind you. When you overtake a slower car you should move back into the left lane, when it is clear, to leave the centre lane free for further overtaking by anyone else. Motorways present prime examples of this very dangerous, inexperienced, even ignorant attitude. It is not unusual to find drivers casually rolling along at 50 mph in the overtaking lanes of a 70 mph motorway. Often there is already another driver in the left-hand lane doing the right thing so the slow car in the outside lane effectively blocks the whole road.

The same thing applies to long steep ascents where a single lane road widens to provide for slow-moving traffic. There are a great many drivers who think that 'slow-moving traffic' applies only to heavy trucks. In this situation, the 45 mph driver will religiously stick to the centre lane, forcing faster cars to overtake on the left. When they do, he will blow his horn and shout abuse, suggesting that they are the drivers in the wrong. No road sense.

In the metropolitan areas many drivers will move from a parked position at the kerb to join a free-moving flow of traffic and having done so, accelerate ever so slowly to the speed of the surrounding traffic. The following cars, even though they may have had plenty of room when the entering car began its move, close the gap very quickly and then are forced to brake to avoid the slow mover. This begins a chain reaction that disturbs the flow of traffic for a hundred metres or more. When you enter a line of traffic from any source, accelerate briskly to the traffic speed. That's road sense.

Then there's the driver who wants to turn right at an intersection with lights. He stops, logically, in the centre lane but he does not yet give a signal. The following car, seeing no signal, assumes that our offending motorist is going straight ahead and falls in behind. Then, when the lights change, the driver at the head of the growing line, puts on his right-hand turn indicator and moves out into the intersection. The drivers in the line astern explode into a fit of righteous pique, and begin to shuffle into the moving lane disrupting traffic all the way down the line. Signalling your intention well ahead is good road sense.

So you can see lack of road sense is a lot more than just speeding and hair-raising driving. The funny part about it is that it's so easy and so satisfying to 'do it right'; and it's so exhausting and humiliating and embarrassing to 'do it wrong'!

SENSITIVITY

In competition driving there is an expression which was originally handed down by the fly boys: 'driving by the seat of your pants'. The expression is practically self-explanatory. It means to drive with such sensitivity and such feel for the car as to anticipate its every movement and react accordingly. While it very largely applies to high speed and high performance driving, it has its application in motoring of every form.

We decided back in Chapter 2 that two of the prerequisites of a good driver were concentration and anticipation. In developing a feel for the car these two basics come to light again. Every driver should develop a sensitivity to the performance of his car: a thorough knowledge of its engine revolution/gear range, its slip and roll factors (more of these later), its best, most economical cruising speed, its reaction under heavy braking, and an understanding of its potential reaction in any given situation. There are so many things. Again, from our experiences at the advanced driving school, there are so many drivers who are 'flying blind'.

For example, we regularly ask students, 'What reaction would you expect from your car if, in an emergency, you had to slap on the brakes very hard in a corner?' Only about 5 per cent of drivers know the answer. So only this very small percentage of drivers could anticipate the reaction of the car to such circumstances, and take any necessary corrective action. It is impossible to generalize here. Almost all cars will respond to such treatment differently. So we ask our students to carry out a simulated exercise which will tell them what happens. And hope, thereafter, that they will remember.

In my early working career I was living and operating from a country centre in New South Wales. I drove a company car and I'd had relatively little experience with high-speed open road driving. On a trip between two country centres I was cruising along at about 110 km/h when a farmer on a tractor drove out from behind a clump of trees straight on to the road in front of me. In the panic that followed I jammed on the brakes. When the car finally stopped, it was in a shallow ditch on the opposite side of the road, facing in the wrong direction. The car was undamaged and I was unhurt but, at the time, I had no explanation for the surprising and unexpected reaction of the car. Later, as opportunities came to try out similar cars under similar conditions, I found that it is a reasonably common reaction. Under such severe braking the weight of the car is suddenly thrust on to the front wheels. The back wheels lose a considerable amount of their traction and with the weight off them they will lock up. Now the locked wheels will slide downhill, down the camber of the road and the car begins to adopt a 'turn right' attitude which will go on and on if unchecked. Had I known this, I could have anticipated the reaction of the car and taken corrective action as I hit the brakes. I was lucky there was no car coming in the opposite direction. Others, in the same situation, might not be so fortunate.

When we talk to drivers about slides and skids and ask them to allow a car to slide deliberately so that they can learn what it feels like and how to control it, we find again that most of them have very little feel for the reaction of the car. Many people will allow the car to get so far into the slide before they react that it is then too late. The reason appears to be that they do not know that the car is sliding until they are galvanized into action by visual stimuli. They have no feel for the car—no sensitivity to its behaviour.

Some examples of the sensitivity one can develop in driving are: The feel for the grip of the front tyres for the road. Such feel is heightened or de-graded by suspension geometry, choice of tyre, steering mechanisms, even the steering wheel itself. In almost all cars there is at least sufficient feel to tell the driver whether or not the tyres are actually gripping the road. A complete loss of front-end traction, for example, is recognised by a sudden loss of this feel together with the sensation of the steering wheel becoming light in the driver's hands. Unfortunately, today's modern trend to cars with power steering has removed from us much of that important characteristic of steering feel. If you become interested in driving and want to do it well you will probably want to avoid artificial devices which 'make driving easier'.

The feel for the brake pedal and its influence upon the brake discs and/or drums is important. The action of the pads or shoes on the brakes is fed back through the hydraulic lines and master cylinder and into the pedal and thus to the driver's foot. The driver can, for example, feel a brake which is out of true because the pedal moves beneath his foot. He can sense the input of too much pressure because when the brake fluid has moved the pads or shoes to the point where they are in contact with the discs or drums it refused to move further and more pressure achieves nothing more than to 'tense' the brake pedal lever. At this point, incidentally, the brakes will have locked the wheels and the driver will be able to feel that with his hands as well (let alone the fact that he can hear it).

The feel for the grip of the rear tyres is transmitted back through the car to the driver's body. He may sense the beginnings of a loss of traction at the rear wheels some tenths of a second before there will be any recognisable visual stimulus. In a long wheelbase car this information takes some time to come forward to the driver's seat but such a car also moves into a slide characteristic relatively slower and thus the driver has time to decipher the information and respond. In a short wheelbase car the transmission of information from rear to front is much faster and, accordingly the driver needs to react much more quickly to control the developing situation.

The mix of roll and pitch (i.e. the motion of the car on its suspension) is informative once you understand the limits of each in the car you drive. Feeling these constant and progressive changes of attitude helps the driver to avoid allowing any of them to become dangerous in their extremes.

When you concentrate on the information the car is constantly providing for you, you begin to understand its language, as a result it is not altogether ridiculous to suggest that you develop the capacity to converse with your car. You 'talk' back to it by responding to its messages, and feeding back input of your own. You and the car become a team, enjoying a physical empathy which helps to keep the pair of you out of trouble.

Cornering:
The Technique

5

CORNERING:
THE TECHNIQUE

Probably within the first mile or so of your first drive you will have had to turn a corner. Assuming that you were travelling quite slowly, the exercise would have presented no problem for you—except that you may have wondered what to do with your hands as the wheel came around. Almost certainly you would not have been aware of the cornering forces at work on the car. Later as you progress with your driving, the process of cornering becomes as routine as any other operation of car handling.

Sometime during your lifetime of driving, however, it will probably be a corner that will give you your worst moment. For drivers who are inclined to 'press on', as most of us are at least occasionally, corners and curves are the greatest natural hazard on the road.

Basically, the process of cornering can be learnt while the car is standing still. You will remember that in Chapter 3 we suggested that the most effective hand position on the steering wheel is at 'quarter to three'. From this position you can turn through 180 degrees without taking either hand from the wheel. Sit in your car and do just that. You will find that your arms begin to cross and eventually that your elbows are almost touching. By this time you will have had to relax the grip of your lower hand slightly, but the upper hand is doing most of the work anyway. The lower hand remains in contact with the wheel and in such a position that it can be brought back into effective use immediately should you need suddenly to straighten the wheel for any reason. If you are sitting squarely behind the wheel you will find that you can turn it an equal amount in either direction and that the amount of turn available is enough for most normal corners and curves, particularly those you will encounter on the open road.

In the cities and suburbs, however, you will be making sharp turns which will require more lock than the 180 degrees available without taking your hands from the wheel. In the city, though, you will not be driving at speeds where cornering alone will be likely to get you into trouble. So you use the 'hand over hand' method of steering. With this method you begin your turn in the method mentioned earlier. When it becomes obvious

that you will need more lock for the turn, you remove the lower hand, replace it at the top of the wheel and continue to pull the wheel around. If this still is insufficient, take the (now) lower hand and again bring it to the top of the wheel. Complete the turn and return the wheel to the straight ahead position by reversing the above or by allowing the wheel to slip back through the hands until you can take up your 'quarter to three' position again.

I mentioned earlier that the foregoing is in direct conflict with the methods of instruction used by most advanced driving organizations and a great many driving instructors the world over. All these people instruct on the technique of steering by using the 'push pull' or 'shuffle' technique. Their reference is the British Hendon Police Driver Training Centre, which for years has been acclaimed as the reference point for all driver training. I will not recommend the 'push pull' method of steering for anyone, save a few partially disabled drivers who cannot lift their arms high enough for 'hand over hand'. I have been through the reasons earlier (see page 28) but I will add that if you have learned the 'push pull' and do it well, don't change back. There is no reason for you to do so.

Having become used to the feel of the wheel and adopted the correct sitting position, the next objective in cornering is to make the process as smooth and as clean as possible. There are three stages in cornering and one all-enveloping technique. The technique is described simply as 'slow in—fast out'. The three stages are: approach to turn point; turn point to clipping point; and clipping point to exit. If any one of these is more important than another it is the first stage. If the approach to a corner is not exactly right the whole of the rest of the corner will be wrong. Let's put it this way. If your approach is right there is a good chance that your exit will also be right; if your approach is wrong you may not exit at all!

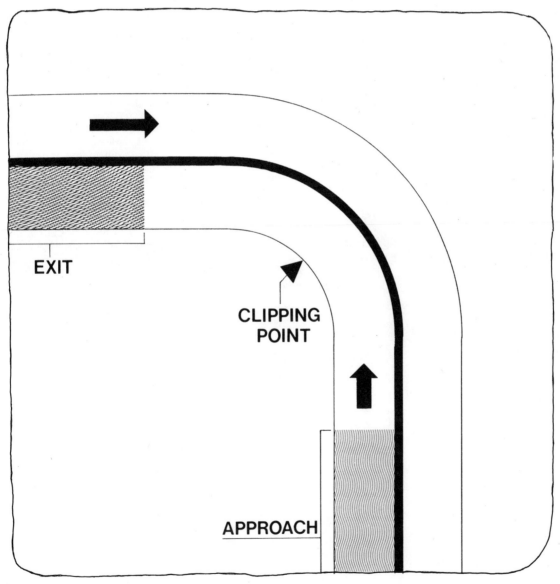

EXIT

CLIPPING
POINT

APPROACH

The segments of a corner

THE APPROACH

In reality, your appro. h to a corner or curve is the same for a 20 mph intersection turn as it is for a 70 mph open highway curve. For obvious reasons the intersection turn requires more than the basic cornering technique because there are other requirements of observation and procedure which must be undertaken at the same time. Nevertheless, the principles of the operation are the same for both.

First of all the driver must evaluate the degree of turn required to negotiate the corner and the speed at which it can safely be taken. He must then bring the car down to that speed, either by braking or by simply taking his foot off the accelerator. If the corner is a slow one, it is desirable to use a lower gear so that maximum available power is at hand for the exit. It is not necessary, or even desirable, to use the gearbox to slow the car for a turn. Brakes are for slowing, gears are for going. So, use the brakes to slow the car, then select the gear you think will best suit your corner.

The reduction of speed, by braking or decelerating, and any necessary down change should be completed before the turn point. The down change can be made later than the speed reduction—just before the turn point. The 'double shuffle' technique should be used to ensure a clean, stable change. In normal cornering procedure there is no point in using the gears to save the brakes as it is more expensive to replace the gearbox than it is to change the brake pads or linings. Using the gearbox to save the brakes is still recommended for long steep descents where the brakes might become overheated unless some assistance is given by engine braking.

When you approach a corner or curve, two points should clearly stand out as being most important: the speed of entry and the stability of the car. Look after one and the other will look after itself. Smooth application of brakes and a clean down change when required will ensure balance and stability at the point of entry into the corner.

There's just one other point that has to be considered and that is 'line'. But that's a subject to be considered independently.

THE CLIPPING POINT

The clipping point of a corner is the point at which the car will come closest to the inside edge of that corner. Somewhere about the clipping point (stage two of the corner or curve) the power is re-applied. The point at which the driver begins to accelerate again depends largely upon the radius of the curve. In a *fast* open curve it can be soon after the turn point, usually well before the clipping point. In a *slow* corner it will be later, certainly not until the car is pointed in the direction of exit, and almost always after the clipping point.

There is a habit among drivers who are travelling quickly on the open highway of wanting to get back on the accelerator again too early. This tends to push the car away from the clipping point and it will be necessary to pull on more steering as you gain speed. After the turn point it is desirable to let the car settle into the corner first. This assists stability and also enables the driver to ensure that he has placed his car correctly for the turn. Once it is clear that the car is settled and well under control, the engine can be put back to work. At this point, and again to maintain smoothness and stable control, the accelerator should be applied gently and squeezed open as the car enters the third stage of the corner.

THE EXIT

If the first and second stages of a corner have been treated with finesse and skill, the third stage is capable of looking after itself. After leaving the exit point, the car, now under progressive acceleration, is directed into the subsequent line of travel and brought up to the desired travelling speed. . .until the next corner comes up.

In the advanced school we found we had to come up with a phrase for cornering by which we could direct students from the passenger's seat. Our directions had to be short, precise and meaningful. To cover the three stages of cornering and the 'slow in—fast out' reference we came up with 'off—turn—squeeze'. Try taking yourself through your own favourite set of corners with the same expression next time you're in your car. I think you'll find it works beautifully. Remember to leave appropriate settling delays between each direction to yourself.

LINE

The easiest way to describe 'line' in a corner is by illustration, so see the diagram on page 37. This represents a somewhat ideal situation; in practice, of course, some flexibility is necessary because of varying road widths and conditions. Suffice to say that you should choose a line for a corner with two purposes in mind. First, the line should straighten the corner as much as possible, to relieve strain on both the suspension and the tyres. Second, a line should allow for a margin of error in the third stage of the corner—just in case you have been inaccurate with your first two stages. You should also attempt to select a line which you can maintain with as little movement of the steering wheel as possible.

The greatest difficulty people seem to experience when trying to establish a line on a curve is that they want to turn too early. If there is any error to be made in selecting a turn point, it is better to turn a little too late than it is to turn too early. For reasons which will become clearer when we come to 'slides and skids' (in Chapter 6), a car which has been committed too early to a corner will tend to run wide at the exit (stage three) of the corner. On most corners the driver has a clear view of the point of entry but not such a view of his projected exit point. For this reason it is important for him to use the road he can see and leave himself a clear margin for error or avoidance in the third stage of the corner.

TRIM

It would be idealistic to believe that a driver will always be accurate with his assessment of speed and radius for a curve. So we need to prepare for the occasions when such accuracy is lacking and when you will need to make mid-corner adjustments to your cornering plan. Such adjustments we call 'trimming' the car.

Generally speaking, a driver who has made an error in his cornering plan, provided the error is not so great as to produce an emergency situation, will adjust such error with the steering wheel, either by turning more tightly or by straightening up slightly. This method of adjustment requires certain physical effort on the part of the driver, and physical effort is also produced within the suspension and tyres of the car, usually resulting in additional and unwarranted strain. It is when the suspension and tyres of a car are under such strain that they are likely to begin to behave badly and the possible resultant loss of adhesion is to be avoided if possible.

The second and more effective method of trimming a car is with the throttle and is known, logically enough, as 'throttle control'. In motor racing circles it is an extensively exploited technique but in road driving most people do not know of it. It is simply a matter of increasing or decreasing throttle pressure sharply, to produce the desired reaction from the car. An increase in throttle pressure in a curve will induce a slight tendency for the car to slip on the front tyres. In this manner the car can be pushed on to a wider line. Thus, if a driver has turned too sharply into a corner and needs to straighten out somewhat, the combination of a gentle straightening of the steering wheel and more acceleration will bring about exactly that reaction. On the other hand, if the car is tending to run wide through the corner and the driver recognizes the need to bring it in more tightly, all he needs to do is lift his foot off the throttle sharply. The resultant transfer of weight back on to the front wheels will tuck the nose in and adjust the line.

There are times when you will need to use some steering wheel to help the throttle trim procedure, but quite often the throttle alone will complete the adjustment and with less stress for both car and driver.

There is a degree of throttle control-ability in every car but it is more pronounced in some than in others. Generally speaking, smaller, more tightly sprung cars are more responsive to throttle control than large, softly sprung cars. The feature is also influenced by the weight of the car, the location of the engine, and the available power. So again we are indicating the need for complete understanding of your vehicle's behaviour patterns. Experimenting with the car on a very quiet or private section of road will show clearly its basic reaction tendencies and will allow you to adjust your driving habits accordingly.

Now that we have the basic cornering plan in mind, let's consider the sort of thing that might happen when something goes wrong with this plan.

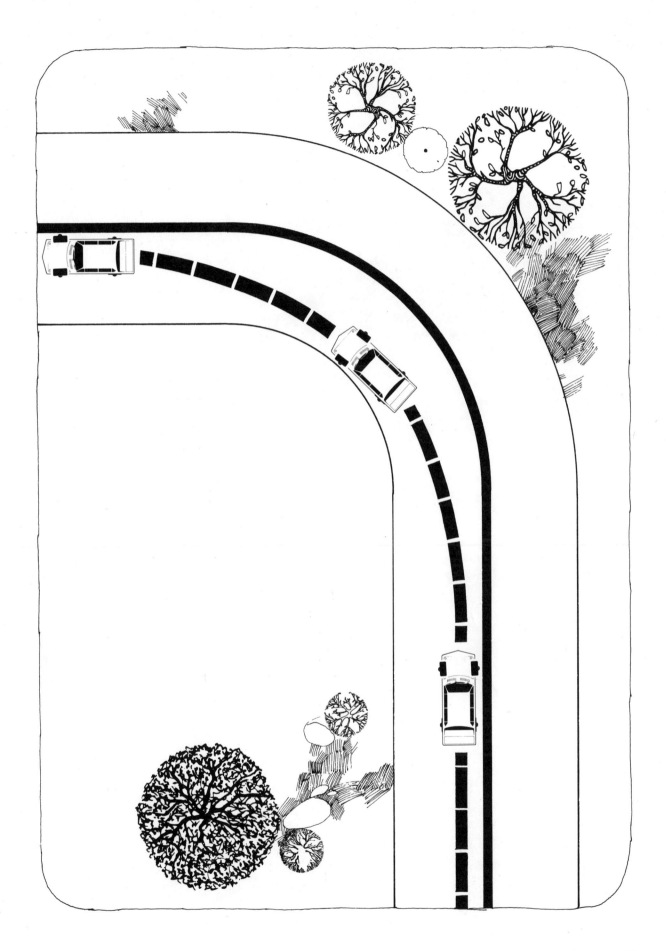

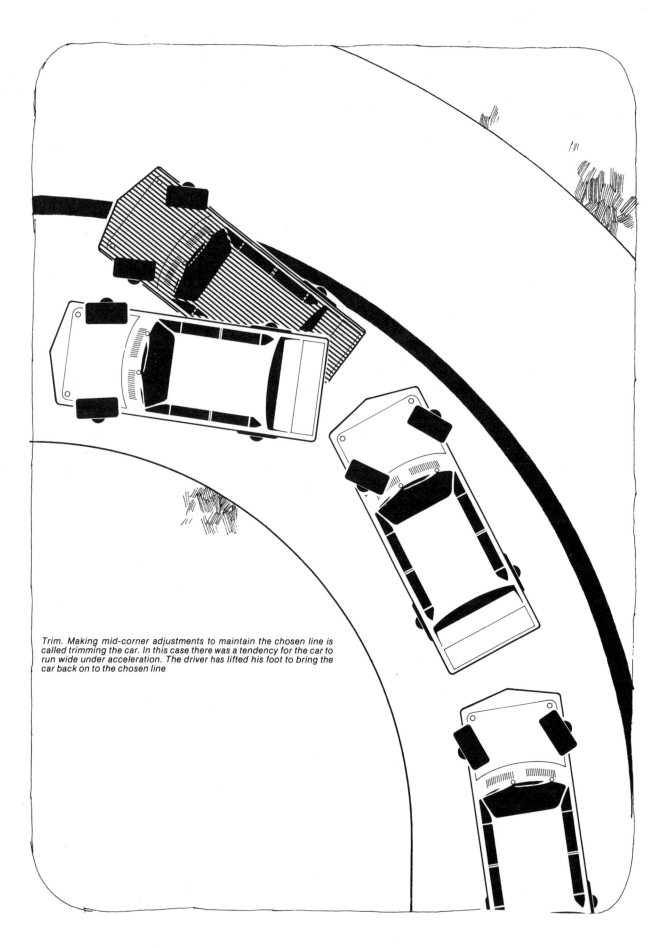

Trim. Making mid-corner adjustments to maintain the chosen line is called trimming the car. In this case there was a tendency for the car to run wide under acceleration. The driver has lifted his foot to bring the car back on to the chosen line

Cornering Problems

6

CORNERING PROBLEMS

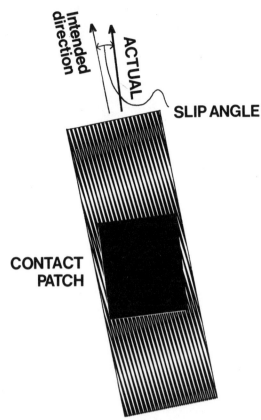

The slip angle is the variation between the direction in which the tyre is pointing and the direction of the contact patch. There is some tread squirm where the tyre meets the road

When a car is driven through a corner or curve it is less stable than when it is travelling in a straight line. It is at this time that suspension travel, body roll, inertia and centrifugal force begin to have their effects upon the car. The driver must learn to recognize and master all of these effects if he is to have complete control over the car at all times. If we go back for a moment to the section on control in Chapter 1 we will recall that the primary form of control a driver should be exploiting is *defensive*. That is, he is at all times attempting to drive in such a way as to avoid potentially difficult situations. However, there are times in every driver's life when he will misjudge the radius of a corner or curve and find himself in the curve at too great a speed for the conditions prevailing at that time, or, when a sudden and unexpected change of road surface (oil, water, gravel, etc.) will bring about a change in the attitude of the car—sometimes a dramatic one.

The car will respond to the situation in a certain manner and the driver must learn to recognize and to control such response. Generally speaking, the most common problem will be some loss of contact between the tyres and the road. At such times the car will slide upon the surface and will not follow the line of the curve chosen by the driver.

Such loss of adhesion is normally referred to as a 'skid' and the terms of reference are generally vague and inaccurate. I would like to explore every possible angle of skid and slide and although this is much more easily described in a car under practical conditions the following should offer a guideline.

Slides and skids occur in a variety of forms. Usually the use of the word *skid* conjures up mental pictures of a wet or slippery road. This in itself is misleading since most forms of slide or skid can occur on dry bitumen or concrete in much the same way as on wet or oily roads, provided the car is travelling fast enough. The first thing I would like to do is to stop using the words 'skid' and 'slide' and refer to all forms of loss of adhesion as 'slip'.

Some degree of slip between tyres and road surface occurs every time the driver turns the steering wheel or applies the brakes. There has not yet been a car/tyre combination developed which will provide 100 per cent adhesion. However the degree of slip under normal conditions is so slight that the driver is not aware that it is happening and certainly it does not present any problem. However, as the speed increases so does the turning and/or braking effort, and with the increase in effort so the slip increases. It is possible for a car to slip on the front wheels more than the back wheels, on the back wheels more than the front wheels or on all four wheels to an approximately equal degree. The driver has to learn to recognize which form of slip is occurring and then apply the appropriate corrective measures.

If you would like to experiment with slip try it this way. The handbook on your car will tell you its static turning circle. Mark two lines on the road exactly that distance apart. Put the left front wheel on one line and execute a very slow 'U' turn and the same wheel will pick up the opposite line. Now repeat the exercise a number of times, each time increasing speed. As the speed builds you will find the left front tyre moves further away from the marked line on each run. That slip is caused by a loss of effective adhesion between tyre and road.

Forces influencing the car

1. Either decelerating or braking, the car transfers its weight to the front, increasing the grip of the front tyres and decreasing the grip of the rear

2. Under acceleration the opposite occurs

3. Body roll occurs in any change of direction. It is possible to combine roll and pitch and thus increase the loss of stability

FRONT WHEEL SLIP

When the front wheels of a car slip more than the rear wheels the car is said to be in a condition of front wheel slip. It is also known as 'understeer', 'front wheel slide' and 'front wheel skid', but the fact that it is slipping on the road surface on the front wheels is all that the driver really needs to know. The front wheel slip condition has only one cause but a number of contributing factors. The cause is excessive speed for a corner or curve for the conditions applying at the time. The contributing factors are listed.

1. *Harsh steering*—that is, the driver has pulled the car too hard into the corner. Smooth, progressive application of steering lock may have avoided the problem.
2. *Harsh braking*—the driver has recognized that he is travelling too fast and braked harshly in fright. The front wheels (all four in fact, but it is the front that is significant) lock momentarily and in this state provide no adhesion.
3. *Road condition*—obviously the degree of front wheel slip will be greater if the road is slippery for any reason, such as water, ice, snow, gravel, oil and so on.
4. *Tyre type and design*—the degree of front wheel slip will also be greater with some tyres than it will with others. See Chapter 9 for a broader explanation. The situation could be worse if the road is slippery as well.
5. *Tyre pressure*—if the pressures of the tyres is not regularly checked and pressures are lower than those recommended (see Chapter 10) then again there will be a greater degree of front wheel slip.
6. *Road shape*—if the road surface is badly cambered, that is, tends to drop away from the front wheels, the slip will tend to increase.

Despite all the above, the main cause of front wheel slip is that the driver is going too fast. But this needs further explanation too. For example, driver A may be driving accurately and well, using the cornering technique described in the previous chapter. He has judged the shape and speed of the approaching corner and set his speed accordingly. He enters the corner and begins to accelerate through; as he does he becomes progressively aware that the car appears to be running wide. Unless he continues to turn the steering wheel further and further the car will not come around on the chosen line. This is a condition of front wheel slip. The tyres have lost some of their grip on the road surface and are not carrying the car in the precise direction which they are pointed. The driver may immediately establish that

(i) he is going too fast—even though the excess may have been only slight,
(ii) he is exaggerating that speed by continuing to accelerate,
(iii) one or other of the above contributing factors is also having its effect.

The driver will eventually react instinctively to the situation. Once he realizes that his continuing application of steering lock is not having the desired effect, he will remove his foot from the accelerator. At this time the weight of the car will transfer from back to front, helping the front wheels to regain their lost traction. The car will then come on to the desired line and the driver will be in a position to resume normal progress (see the section on trim on page 36).

Front wheel slip. For one or other of the reasons described in the text, the car has an excessive degree of slip at the front wheels, and does not provide sufficient response to the driver's steering commands. It is in fact understeering the corner

Now let's take a second driver, B, and set him up in similar but more exaggerated circumstances. This driver is in a hurry. He is approaching the same corner at a greater speed and he intends to get around it as quickly as possible. He prepares for the corner in the same way as the first driver, makes his entry and again begins to accelerate through. But his acceleration is harder, since he is hurrying. The front wheel slip attitude becomes apparent earlier and again the driver tries to correct by turning harder. However, since the wheels are slipping on the road surface, the steering responds only slightly and the car continues to want to run wide. Again he instinctively lifts off the accelerator and again the weight transfer is effected, but this time more violently. The front wheels regain their traction but the transfer of weight has been of such degree that the rear wheels lose their grip and the car begins to spin around its front axis. The driver has removed the problem of front wheel slip but initiated a secondary problem situation. We will leave this driver in a state of suspended animation for a while and come back to him later.

A third driver, C, on the same corner has misjudged the speed of the corner completely and entered, let's say, 20 mph too fast. At the point of entry he recognizes that he is going too fast, and in a fright/panic situation jumps hurriedly on the brakes. His braking is excessively harsh, however, and the front wheels lock. There is an immediate loss of traction and the car tends to go straight ahead with no response to the steering whatsoever.

Statistics on single car accidents on corners of this type clearly indicate two ultimate possibilities: either the driver freezes at this point, probably because no further effective message came through as to what he should do to correct the situation; or his momentum at the moment of braking was such that there was not enough time for him to take corrective action.

If the latter occurred then he is about to have some sort of collision. If the former, that is, if he had time to react but did not know what to do, he should have released some of his braking pressure in an attempt to get the front wheels rolling again. But, since the weight would have been on the front wheels, as they began to roll again the car would have begun to follow the direction of the steering wheels. There would still be considerable momentum influencing the car, however, so the tail would have begun to slide outwards as happened to driver B.

Let's assume driver C managed to get adhesion on the front wheels again, and leave him with driver B in the suspended state where his car is beginning to spin.

Rear wheel slip: The driver is correcting by pointing the front wheels in the direction of intended travel

Rear wheel slip: The end result is a complete spin

REAR WHEEL SLIP

By now it will be obvious that the whole business of slip is somewhat more complicated than most instructors would have you believe. That is, if they mention the subject at all.

Rear wheel slip is the opposite of front wheel slip in that the rear wheels have lost a greater degree of adhesion than the front wheels. The causes and contributing factors for rear wheel slip are essentially the same as those which affect front wheel slip, except that an additional cause of rear wheel slip is harsh acceleration late in a corner—but this added cause only affects rear wheel drive cars. You see what I mean by complicated!

Basically, what determines whether a car will slide on the front wheels or the rear wheels is car design and balance, usually factors over which the owner has no control other than by modifying his car. Cars with engines in the front generally slip on the front wheels; cars with engines in the back generally slip on the rear wheels. But this is not a hard and fast rule and drivers should find some way of testing their cars to find out exactly what condition can be expected in case of that unexpected emergency.

You will already have noticed that when we left two of our front wheel slip drivers, they were in a certain amount of trouble with the rear wheels beginning to slip and the car beginning to spin. In each case they had effectively managed to remove the front wheel slip problem, only to be confronted with a second problem of similar magnitude. We will leave them yet again briefly while we examine a fourth case on the same corner.

Driver D is also approaching too fast but somewhere earlier in his driving experience he has learned what happens when one jumps on the brakes in such a corner. He knows what he should not do but he does not yet know what he should do. So he is heading into the corner with his foot off the accelerator and off the brake, that is, in a trailing throttle condition. The car is reasonably well balanced at this time but, despite this, the momentum of his speed of entry will cause a loss of adhesion and most commonly this loss will be on the rear wheels, meaning that the car will begin to spin. Thus he is now in the same situation as drivers B and C (although through different circumstances) and we can now begin to relieve all three drivers of their developing problem.

In a real wheel slip situation caused by excessive speed of entry into a corner, the influencing factor is momentum (or inertia if you prefer the pure physics). The car has a strong tendency to want to continue on in the direction it was last travelling. The driver's aim must be to provide some counteracting force which will change the direction of travel of the car. First, however, he needs to control the developing spin situation which, if left to increase in intensity, would have the car careering off the road backwards, or in cases of slightly lower speed, spinning inwards, but equally off the road. Therefore, the first action on the driver's part is to check the degree of slip.

To do this the driver must change the direction in which his front wheels are pointing. Let's clarify this. Think a moment about drivers B, C and D and imagine yourself in their cars. In any of the three cases described you have taken certain procedures which have resulted in your car beginning to spin about its front axis. Let's say that the corner was a left-hander. As the tail slides outwards the car begins to turn harder left; in a fraction of a second it will be pointing in towards the edge of the road. It is almost as though you have turned too hard for the corner and the car is 'oversteering'. Certainly then you do not need to continue to keep the wheels pointed to the left because that's going to make things worse. If you had in fact been *turning* too hard

45

for the corner, what you would have done is to begin to straighten the wheels, possibly even turn them slightly to the right to put you back on line again.

In this case the rear of your car is sliding outwards and producing the same effect so you need to straighten the wheels and possibly begin to turn slightly to the right. In other words you turn in the direction of the slide as all the good motoring books will tell you.

In most cases, however, that's as far as the books go. They do not tell you how much to turn in the direction of the slide. So, as the tail slides out you get something of a surprise, possibly even a fright, and you react by violently swinging the wheel over on to opposite lock. The car reacts equally violently. Now your wheels are pointed hard right and since that is the direction of travel the front wheels are barely slipping at all. Because they have near maximum adhesion the car will begin to follow them. Since the rear wheels have virtually no adhesion they will simply follow suit; they will flick back to straight ahead and continue slipping into a slide in the opposite direction. The situation is called 'over-correction', but I prefer 'over-reaction', since the driver simply over-reacted to the developing spin.

Still complicated? Come back to the point where the tail is swinging outwards and you want to stop it. Control your fright if you can (practice helps—find a quiet dirt road); turn the steering wheel back to straight ahead and then point the wheels as near as you can in the direction in which you wish to go. Now the car will respond. But all that will happen so far is that the tail will stop whipping around. The whole car will move sideways now because it is still being influenced by the momentum. So at the same time you squeeze back on the accelerator, which has the effect of transferring the weight to the back and pushing the rear tyres harder on the road. As they begin to grip again, the car will start to move forward and you can then adjust your steering accordingly to keep the car travelling in the direction you wish to go.

For every form of speed-induced rear wheel slip condition, regardless of other influencing factors, the corrective procedure is the same. Turn the front wheels exactly in the direction in which you wish to travel and squeeze on the accelerator. But there are still little tricks to watch for. Remember, if you can, not to be harsh with your steering. The same applies to your throttle control. If you are driving a rear wheel drive car, harsh acceleration at this point will cause the rear wheels to slip more (the sudden application of power will produce wheelspin). If you are driving a front wheel drive car, harsh acceleration will pull the car back straight and push it into a front wheel slip condition again and you will have to go through the whole procedure once more. You don't always have enough time or area to do it all again.

While we are on the subject of time, keep in mind that all of what I have been describing happens in seconds, in fact, in fractions of seconds in some cases. Therefore your actions must be fast—but they must also be very smooth. Again, practice is the only answer. You could say, if you like, that you are not going to bother to practise, that you'll just slow down a bit instead. But even so, slowing down will be no guarantee that you will never misjudge the radius, shape or condition of a corner. It's better to be able to handle it than it is just to hope it won't ever happen.

Rear wheel slip. For one or other of the reasons described in the text, the car has developed a rear wheel slip attitude which, unchecked, will cause it to spin into the opposite lane of traffic or within its own lane or off the road on the inside of a curve. It is oversteering the corner

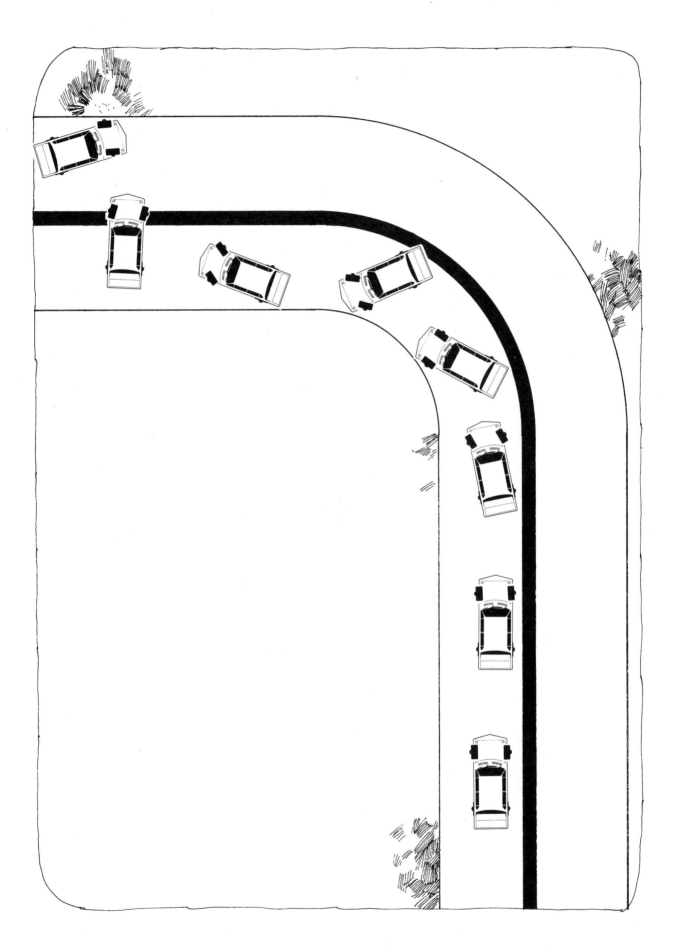

There is one more form of rear wheel slip we need to think about and we have already touched on it very briefly. Earlier I said that if you were driving a car with rear wheel drive and you accelerated too harshly while attempting to correct a speed-induced rear wheel slip situation, you would increase the slip condition because of wheelspin. Imagine yourself now, on a wet day, making an entirely conventional left-hand turn in the suburbs. Your speed is down to 15 mph, perhaps less, but as you complete the turn and begin to accelerate away from the corner you feel the tail of the car begin to slip across the road. You will instinctively lift your foot from the throttle again and the car will settle back and run true. Your instinctive 'lift off' cured the problem because it was caused by your excessive acceleration in the first place. You had put on more power than the rear tyres could handle on the slippery road and the wheels spun. Again, you might have reacted in fright by flinging the steering wheel around to put on opposite lock, in which case the car would have gripped as soon as you removed your foot from the accelerator and taken off in the direction you were pointing it. But if you respond quickly enough, there is normally no need for steering correction here. Just lifting your foot will cure the problem. But if you do correct, that is, turn the front wheels in the direction of intended travel, make sure you do so smoothly.

Violent overcorrection of a rear wheel slip condition will almost certainly produce a slide in the opposite direction

BRAKING AND SLIP

There is a logical conclusion to all this which brings down the wrath of the motoring gods every time I suggest it. Almost all of the foregoing control techniques for rear wheel slip require training and practice. You could go to a school and learn the method of control thoroughly and then not be required to use it for, say, ten years. How much do you think you might be able to recall in that mini-second you have to respond to the developing emergency? There is a reasonable chance you are already shaking your head in doubt. And I agree with you.

Naturally enough, the logical suggestion to make is that you should not get into such a situation in the first place but as we've already decided, that's also somewhat unrealistic. So there has to be another way. Imagine yourself confronted with a sudden and unexpected rear wheel slip condition. Assume, on this occasion, the car has begun to spin and you feel there is little hope of catching it. The only thing left for you to do is to stop it. Yet you have probably been told many times about the dangers of 'braking in a skid', so a brief moment of confusion exists. In that moment, while you delay, all hope of control is lost and the car crashes. Sadly it also crashes while it is still travelling quite fast (20 mph is fast if you hit a tree). If you had not hesitated and had put the brakes on quickly once you had accepted that you had little chance of controlling the gyrating car you may still have crashed—but you would have crashed more slowly. In fact, in almost any moment of potential danger your every instinct calls out for you to stop the car and it is only the inhibitions of inadequate training that stop you from taking such positive action. Actually the fear of braking a sliding car is unfounded. It is based on a belief that the car will roll over under such conditions, but that is not necessarily true. Nearly all modern cars are quite stable under conditions of slide. They need to be tripped over, literally, to roll. So, for as long as your sliding car maintains the established road surface, the chances of its rolling are remote. It will simply slide to a stop.

49

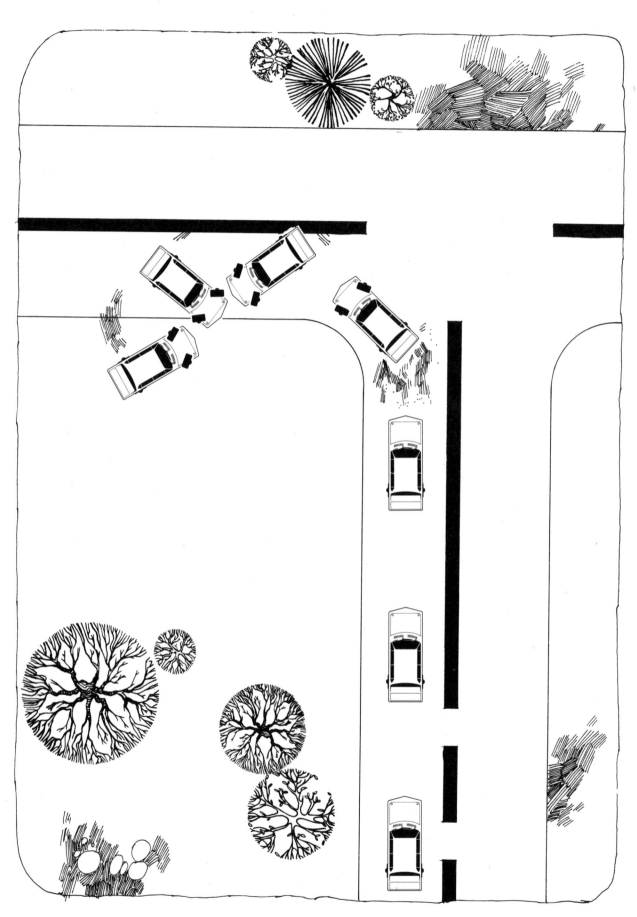

The driver has braked hard enough to lock the back wheels—the back of the car slides down the camber

Controlled braking should produce no directional instability

If you now take this thought one step further you will soon realize that it is even reasonably possible to predict where the car will finish up at the end of its wild slide. Think about it like this. The car in its rear wheel slip situation is sliding at the back wheels. Chances are the front wheels still have fairly good traction. So the car is pivoting. If you jump on the brakes hard and lock the wheels you will have little or no influence on the back wheels since they are already sliding, but you will break traction on the front wheels; now all four wheels will be sliding. Except for the influence of momentum (the rear wheels having something of a start on the front wheels), the car should now be sliding equally on all four wheels. When the front wheels catch up to the back wheels as far as their momentum is concerned that's exactly what will be happening. Thus it is possible for you to direct (with surprising accuracy at times) the final stopping place of the car simply by deciding when to hit the brakes. If you look at the diagram you'll see what I mean. The potential end result (favourable) is that the car will spin once only, on its own side of the road, and then stop, and you will escape with nothing more than a red face. The potential end result (unfavourable) is that you will still crash (which there is a better than even money chance you would have done anyway) but at least your final impact speed will be slower.

Actually, in *any* situation where you have reason to believe that you have lost control of the car, stop it as fast as you possibly can!

Just to illustrate that line of thinking, if you have ever watched a motor race meeting you may have seen examples of the above situations. One driver in a wild slide madly over-corrects, and then slams into an Armco fence when the secondary reaction catches up with him; another, who recognizes his loss of control, instantly brakes to a stop. The second driver may be embarrassed, but at least he has the chance to ride again; the first has an expensive repair bill at the very least.

The best answer to all the various problems of slip and slide is to try to develop a very high degree of sensitivity to the subtle movements of your car. It is better to catch a small problem than let it develop into a big one. Yet most drivers are so insensitive that the problem has become a big one before they are able to recognize that anything is happening.

Once, I interviewed a number of top racing drivers for a television show and I asked them all how they knew when they were going too fast into a corner. None of them could provide an answer that made any real sense and as I thought about it later I began to see why. These drivers were all practitioners, not theorists. They knew what they were required to do only because of their vast experience. They had learned long ago to live with their cars, to feel every movement, every ripple, even a minute degree of slip. They had learned to feel for adhesion and to know accurately when the degree of slip was becoming greater than was reasonable. They took it for granted that most people had this talent to some degree and were surprised when people crashed as a result of spinning a car on the road.

But the average driver has never felt a slide of any type until one catches him by surprise and puts him into a ditch. Even then it usually happens so fast that he learns nothing from it except that it's not a very pleasant experience. This is one reason why some form of competition driving is so strongly recommended for today's drivers. It helps develop this sensitivity. It also offers a relatively safe outlet for the desire to have a bit of speed now and then.

The power slide has the car in a rear wheel slip situation because the back wheels are spinning

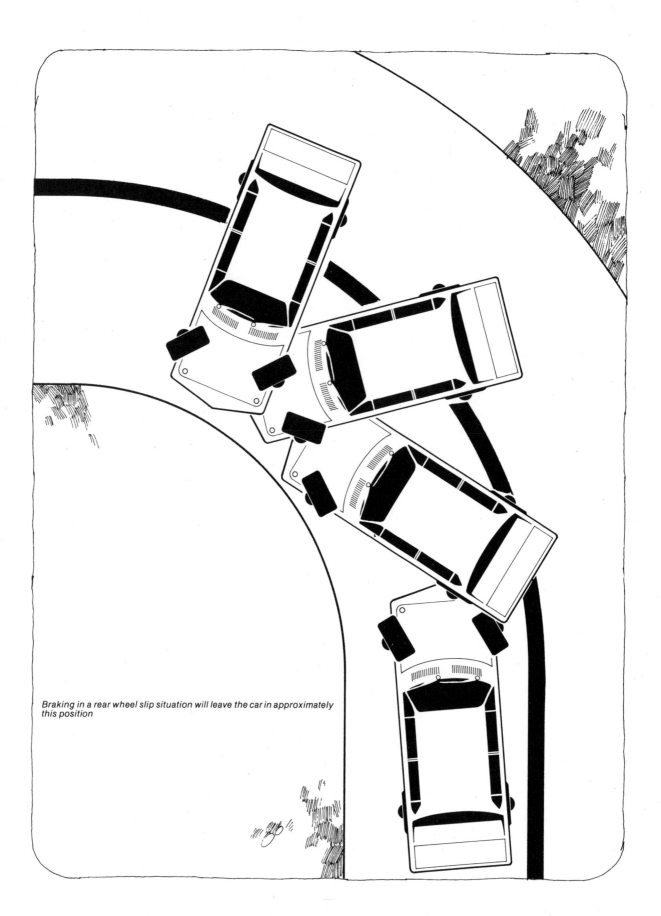

Braking in a rear wheel slip situation will leave the car in approximately this position

Specifics of Car Control

7

SPECIFICS OF CAR CONTROL

Although cornering and its associated problems are likely to cause you the greatest difficulties with your driving there are obviously other points which require knowledge and understanding as well. All of them are significant in developing an overall system of car control. They include aspects of driving in which you will be involved every time you get behind the wheel. On most occasions, under conditions of normal driving, none of them is likely to present any hazard. However, there will be times where conditions will not be normal and where an emergency or potential emergency is rapidly developing.

BRAKING
The function of the brakes on a car is to slow down the wheels. Obviously, this in turn slows the car but it is important to think of the brakes slowing the wheels because, ideally, all four wheels should slow at the same rate. It's very rarely that they do, however, and this factor of different rates of braking causes the many problems.

The reasons for uneven braking are simple. In the first place, designers have not yet introduced an effective method of ensuring that all four wheels slow at the same rate. Secondly, even if they had, it would be up to you and your garageman to ensure that the whole system was kept in perfect working order. The most common problem is one which could and should have been eliminated years ago. When you apply the brakes in your car the weight of the car effectively transfers to the front. The back wheels, relieved of a large proportion of their load, will lock up simply because they are flopping about in mid-air, so to speak. This problem can be removed at the design stage by building in either a proportioning valve or a pressure limiting valve which will regulate the amount of pressure being fed into the rear brake system.

The second problem is one of maintenance. Leaking cylinders, dirt or rust on discs or drums, worn pads or linings, different pad or lining material on any wheel or set of wheels, will all contribute to uneven rates of braking. Maintenance is your responsibility.

Probably if you have ever had trouble slowing a car, it will have been on a wet road where sudden application of the brakes can cause loss of traction on the front, on the rear, or perhaps on all four wheels. Then you will have found two things. Pushing the brakes harder does nothing to help the stopping action and turning the steering wheel produces no response by way of a change of direction. It's a frightening situation. So far as the wet or slippery surface is concerned, it can be avoided by allowing considerably more room between cars than you normally would, or controlled by easing the pressure off the brake pedal until the wheels unlock and gain traction again. Of course, if the latter course is the only one left to you, you will have to be prepared to take very sudden avoiding action once the wheels have regained their traction. The mere fact of having taken off some of the braking pressure will have increased your stopping time and distance.

There is a problem, less common, which occurs under harsh braking on dry adhesive surfaces as well. It will usually occur only at high speeds and consequently is the more dangerous. It is also more common in the 'ordinary family saloon' than in the more expensive and exotic class of car. When a driver brakes in an emergency or even a potential emergency he usually does so in a state of momentary fright. Thus his application of the brake is harsh and violent. The sudden transfer of weight combined with the locking rear wheels will almost always cause a loss of directional stability. Uncontrolled, this will almost certainly mean a spin, as described in Chapter 6.

Ideally, no one should ever panic when going for the brakes—but that's unrealistic. Fright is the most difficult human emotion of all to control. And, in a car, the one most likely to cause problems.

---

1. *Uncontrolled emergency braking can result in complete loss of directional stability*

2. *Even if the car does begin to turn, it can be caused to maintain its desired track by using the steering wheel to correct*

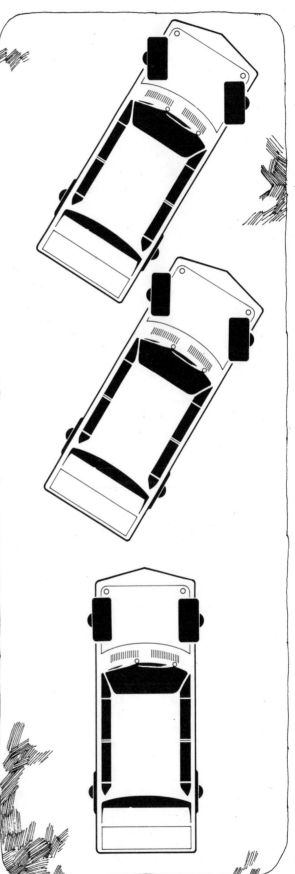

The ideal reaction is for the driver to get his foot to the brake pedal as quickly as he can and then squeeze the pedal hard up to the point of wheel lock up. Then a very slight easing of the pressure will remove the lock up, allowing the wheels to roll again and the brakes to operate at maximum retardation. The nearer a driver can come to this ideal the better, but this will largely depend on his personality. However, let's assume he has leapt hard on the brakes. Once the initial fright has exercised its effect and before the instability caused by sudden braking takes over completely, he should ease the pressure slightly to get the wheels rolling again, and then squeeze again to lock-up point.

A bad habit with most drivers is that when the brakes do lock up the wheels, they take the offending foot right off the brake and start again, usually with the same result. There is no need. All that is required is that the pressure be eased slightly to release the locked wheel or wheels.

Learning to control brake lock up is by no means easy. It requires a great deal of practice, enough, in fact, to establish a conditioned reflex. You work at the problem so hard and so often that when the moment of crisis comes you are conditioned to react correctly, and your reflex action overcomes your fright reaction. Try thinking of it this way. Let's say that your car will lock its wheels if you apply say, 300 kilopascals (43.5 lb/in²) of pressure to the pedal. Theoretically, then, it will not lock its wheels if you apply 290 kilopascals (42 lb/in²) of pressure. You are going to have to find out how far you can depress the pedal before the 300 kilopascals point is reached. In the first instance, it's a measure of distance. Perhaps you establish that the pedal will lock the wheels when you move it 10 centimetres. So you must try to establish how much pedal resistance there is beneath your foot at that 10 centimetre point. As you work at it you will develop a feel for that resistance and also for the distance of travel of your foot. Eventually you can get to the point where you can apply brakes very quickly and move your foot, say, only 9 centimetres, at which point you will have close to maximum braking effort without lock up,

which, in fact, is the ideal situation.

The great temptation that must be resisted then is to push harder, specially when, on initial application, the car doesn't seem to be stopping fast enough. Pushing the pedal harder will achieve nothing but locked wheels. You will realize after a while (and assuming that you keep your braking system in the best possible condition) that although the initial stopping reaction does not seem to be brilliant, the slowing effect increases as speed is lost.

There could be some debate as to whether 'distance' or 'control' is more important in an emergency braking exercise. For my money, it is 'control' you need, always. As it happens, with control you will also get distance whereas with distance you may not necessarily have control. To explain. On a dry road of good surface the car will stop in about the same distance whether the brakes have locked the wheels or whether the wheels are still rolling. Which would suggest that hanging in on the brakes to the point of locking the wheels is not so disastrous as it seems. On a wet road however (or on loose gravel) the locked wheels will simply go on sliding down the road, with a substantial increase in stopping distance. So firstly, practising brake control will help to make it a habit to always do it right. Secondly there is the point of loss of directional stability. Until it becomes compulsory for all car manufacturers to limit the degree of lock-up potential with pressure limiting devices, the rate of lock will be uneven on some cars. If the back wheels lock first there is a very good chance that the car will slide tail first down the camber of the road, thus pointing the front of the car in entirely the wrong direction. Alternatively, if the front wheels lock the car will be unsteerable and it will be impossible for you to take avoiding action should it happen that you are not able to stop in time. So you can see why I advocate brake control to avoid locking wheels wherever and whenever possible.

BRAKE FAILURE

Although it is relatively unusual in modern cars, complete failure of the foot brake system is a possibility and, understandably, it seems to be the emergency people fear most. Obviously if total brake failure occurs there has to be an alternative method of bringing the car to a stop.

If there is time, this is not so difficult. At high speeds, say above 50 mph, the driver should change back at least one gear in a manual car and then ease on the hand brake. When the hand brake is effectively slowing the car the next lower gear should be selected, and so on until the car can safely be pulled to the side of the road. In an automatic, all that is required is that the selector should be slipped to Low and then the hand brake used as above. In most cases the gearbox will not immediately engage low range but as the handbrake slows the car, the lower gear will become effective.

But if there is no time for all this, then you have a real emergency and some sort of entanglement with the surrounding countryside would appear to be inevitable. If it is inevitable, it should be deliberate rather than accidental. As soon as the driver becomes aware that he has lost brakes, let's say on a long downhill run, he should steer the car broadside against a kerb or embankment and hope that the friction of contact will slow the car. In a corner, it is better to try to get around the corner than it is to let the car go straight ahead. If you are going too fast for the corner, chances are the car will spin and the act of spinning will itself take off a considerable amount of speed if not all of it. It all sounds very hair raising and it is. But under such circumstances you have two choices—do something or do nothing. To my way of thinking it is better to try anything than nothing at all.

Ultimately, you can spin the car deliberately. Such a practice is for an absolute last ditch effort only but, since it may just save your life, it has to be worth knowing. The technique only applies where you drive a car which has an emergency (hand) brake which operates on the back wheels. The procedure simply requires that you pull on a small amount of steering lock to get the car turning slightly and then pull on the handbrake hard enough to lock the back wheels. The car will immediately spin and in spinning will reduce its speed surprisingly fast. Such a procedure obviously needs a piece of clear road. But in a brakeless car with a dangerous situation coming up at the very least it might reduce the impact of the impending collision.

THE PRE-READING TECHNIQUE

The importance of understanding what is about to happen with the road ahead cannot be over-emphasized. Earlier, I mentioned the desirability of being able to make normally unpredictable circumstances predictable. The pre-reading technique assists to a large extent in doing this.

It applies to all road conditions and situations but more specifically to open road driving. The pre-reading technique is simply the art of determining in advance what you can expect in the next half mile of road. In the city this means that you should alert yourself to major intersections, traffic lights, halt signs and so on well before you get to them. Taking as an example a line of traffic in a right-hand turn lane and a clear road in the straight ahead lane, you would determine well ahead that the road into which the right turn cars are turning will be at least partly obscured from your vision by the cars themselves. You would therefore have to assume, since they must give right of way, that a car or cars could well be turning out of that road into your street, even though you may not see such cars until you are very close to them. Your pre-reading technique will warn you to slow down and be ready to give way yourself.

The technique applies to hundreds of conditions on the road and can be broadly covered in one of the basics which we considered earlier—*observation*. But it is more than just observing. In effect it is anticipating. It is predicting that something unforeseen could happen and preparing for it. On the open highway where speeds are invariably higher it is most important. The fact that you may appear to have the road to yourself does not mean that you do. Every section of the road that you cannot see may present a new hazard and you

Overtaking: Too close for adequate vision, not enough room to accelerate to passing speed

Overtaking: Adequate vision room to move

must be prepared for them. You cannot see into dips or over crests so obviously it would be wrong for you to approach either with your foot on the accelerator. Lift off and have your foot hovering over the brake pedal and you will have saved half your normal reaction time if you should need to slow or stop suddenly. Try reading the curve of the road well before you enter a corner. If you can't be sure of its radius, go in much slower than you would otherwise.

On country roads, don't use telegraph poles to judge the curve of the road. They may follow the line of the road for miles and just when you are beginning to depend on them they will march straight off across a paddock while the road turns sharply.

OVERTAKING WITH SAFETY

On most roads passing another vehicle means taking your car into the opposite traffic lane. The dangers here are obvious. Of all driving manoeuvres, overtaking will require the most judgement. You must be able to accurately assess such details as the distance to be covered before regaining your own traffic lane, the amount of time this will take, the speed of any approaching car, the distance of clear vision and, if you are approaching from well back, the speed of the car you are about to overtake. Again there is a simple basic rule: if in doubt—*don't!* Unless you are absolutely sure that the manoeuvre will be completely safe, do not attempt it. There will always be another opportunity. But it is equally important, once you have made up your mind, that you make your move quickly and precisely. Don't ever loiter about half way between going and not going. When you decide to move, put your foot down hard on the accelerator and keep it there until you can see the car you have overtaken in your rear vision mirror. Then you will be able to move across safely in front and maintain your previous speed.

There is a point about your approach which is also important. When you are travelling noticeably faster than the car in front and it is obvious quite early that you will want to overtake him, don't move up quickly with your foot hard down assuming that everything will be clear when you get close enough. If the road is not clear you will have to brake hard and untidily to tuck yourself back in on your own side of the road. Rather, slow a little as soon as you see the car ahead, determine his speed, check for oncoming traffic. If you cannot move, slow further and do not close up on the car in front. Stay back far enough to be able to accelerate nearly to your passing speed before you move into the opposite lane. First, your vision is less obscured from a reasonable distance, and second, you will be able to complete the passing move more quickly from not having to make a dead start in the wrong lane. If you find occasionally that people speed up when you go to overtake, remember this when someone wants to pass you. It is a very dangerous practice—*never* do it under any circumstances. Let them pass—you have no justification for trying to stop them or for making it difficult. If someone does it to you, drop back in behind as soon as you notice that he has begun to accelerate and wait to see what he does. He may elect to drive faster than he had been, which will perhaps mean that you no longer need to overtake. If he slows down again wait until you have a very clear run before you try to repass—you will need all the room you can get.

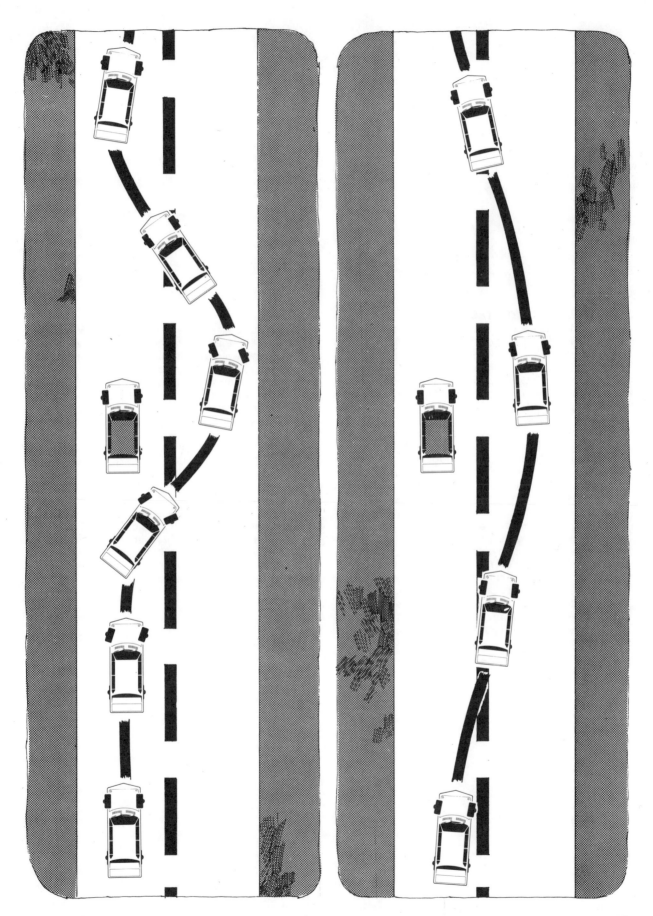

THE 'SPACE CUSHION' TECHNIQUE

While on the subject of needing all the room you can get, it is as well for us to consider the benefits of making such philosophy a standing rule. In motor racing the obvious practice, if you are to be successful, is to get as close to your competitors as you can. In motor racing, however, a driver can be certain that the other driver he is running 'in tandem' with is an expert, highly skilled driver. How does this apply on the road? My recommendation is that every driver you meet in any conditions must be considered to be totally inexpert and for this reason your policy should be precisely the reverse of that of the racing driver. You must endeavour to keep as far away from all other drivers as practicable. There is a standing recommendation to leave one complete car length between you and the motorist ahead for every 10 mph of speed. If we examine this it becomes apparent that it is a very reasonable request. A car travelling at 40 mph is covering the ground at 16 metres per second. With an average braking efficiency of 80 per cent a car will stop from 40 mph in 14 metres. This would be excellent if it were possible for you to hit your brakes at exactly the same instant as the man in front of you. However, reaction plays a major part here. Most people have a reaction time of about 0.5 seconds under ideal conditions.

This presupposes that you have been concentrating to the fullest on the job of driving. At half a second reaction time you will have travelled over 7 metres before you even touch the brake. Add this to your stopping distance and you can see that it will take 21 metres or more to stop. If you were any closer to the man in front than 7 metres you cannot avoid hitting him. So you can realize the necessity for staying your correct distance behind him. Circumstances may cause slight adjustments here and there, however. If you are driving in a continuous stream of slow moving traffic you would have to drive closer to the man in front than usual. But the principle still applies. In traffic you must still have that margin for error or emergency. A standard of 3 metres seems reasonable and it would be as well for you to make a personal rule on this. Never get closer than 3 metres to any car anywhere except when parking. Then you have a space cushion. Just one other point—when it is wet, double the standing rule. Your tyres just might not grip as well as those of the man in front.

Difficult Conditions

8

DIFFICULT CONDITIONS

Almost every driver worth his salt will, at one time or another, want to get away from it all. In most countries of the world, to varying degrees, this will mean getting off the beaten track. And even when that doesn't apply it could still mean an occasional tussle with rain, ice or snow, or all three. For some people, such conditions are a regular fact of life. What I'm getting around to saying is that everyone needs to be constantly prepared for the worst possible road conditions. Coping with such problem conditions can present real difficulties and although for some situations there will be an overlap of control information I think it's worth looking at each possibility individually.

WATER

Rain is by far the most common of all driving hazards. Even in moderate rain, two immediate problems occur which require added care and attention. First, the wet road provides reduced adhesion; second, the wet windscreen reduces visibility. There are, of course, varying degrees of wet from the newly damp road to that which is so wet the water actually flows across it, and finally to actual flood conditions.

In the first instance it is as well to be aware that a newly damp road is quite often the most hazardous of all, especially if that rain comes after a period of dry. The first moisture floats out of the microtexture of the road surface all that fine dirt, oil and rubber which has been accumulating there for weeks. The resultant paste is almost as treacherous as ice. The first step in controlling the potential dangers of such a situation is to be aware of them. When it begins to rain it would not be unrealistic to suggest that one needs to be over-cautious. This means, more than ever, driving gently and smoothly. Do not over-react to anything. Brake lightly and smoothly; accelerate lightly and smoothly; steer gently and smoothly; and of course, travel at reduced speeds. To control acceleration, stay in the highest gear you can get away with in a manually geared car. In an automatic it is possible with most modern systems to engage second gear and thus lock out both low and high. This will help with more gentle acceleration and

some degree of engine braking. If you get any kind of wheelspin (and you should be feeling for it), reduce the degree of acceleration immediately to allow the wheels to roll again. Give yourself added braking margins but then, having done so, feel for wheel lock up, and when it occurs reduce braking pedal pressure to the point where the wheels roll again.

Once again, we're on the subject of sensitivity and that's precisely what this sort of condition needs.

As the rain increases that disastrous chemical paste will eventually be washed away and things should improve. If you have good quality tyres, you should have little trouble with normal rainfall provided that you bear in mind that you have less adhesion potential. Don't overdo things. Continue to drive gently and smoothly. But you can relax a bit; you are in less danger.

If the rain increases in intensity or if it rains for a long period, a new danger will develop. As the water begins to flow across the road or to lie about in puddles, you will be confronted with the possibility of 'aquaplaning' or 'hydraplaning'. These both mean the same thing, but different people give the characteristic different names. The condition occurs when the tyres roll a wall of water ahead of them and ultimately ride up on to that wall of water. Even though this may occur for only a second or so, it will mean that for that amount of time you have no contact with the road whatsoever and therefore nil adhesion. You'll know when it happens because the car will obviously not respond to brakes, steering or power and there is nothing you can do but wait until the car ceases to aquaplane and you can recover control.

The tendency for a tyre to aquaplane increases as the speed of the car increases and is also influenced by the air pressure in the tyre. Thus the lower the pressure and the higher the speed, the greater the chances of an aquaplaning situation. Contrary to general popular belief, one should increase tyre pressures for better control in the wet and, obviously I should think, reduce speed. The higher tyre pressure opens the tread pattern somewhat and also tends to round off the contact patch, giving the tyre a better chance to penetrate the water and find the road beneath.

The ultimate wet condition of course is a flood. It is possible to drive through quite deep water with little trouble if you prepare for it. In the first place if the water is, say, only 20 to 30 centimetres deep (and you should establish the depth of water always before attempting to move the car) you simply drive through very slowly, to avoid creating a bow wave which will swamp the engine, and slightly slipping the clutch, to allow high engine revs and low speed so that you avoid the possibility of stalling in the middle of it all.

If the water is deeper (and how deep depends pretty much on your car, but as a general rule above 60 centimetres is too deep to try), you will need to prepare as follows. Remove the fan belt so that the spinning fan will not throw water all over the engine and drown it. Spray the plugs, high tension leads and electrical contacts with aerosol de-watering fluid and, if you can, wrap them in plastic or similar waterproof material. Find a piece of rubber tube which will go over the exhaust pipe, lead it to a point on the car which will be well above water level and secure it. Walk through the water first to check the route and make sure there are no deep holes. Now drive through as before, slowly, slipping the clutch.

In all instances of driving through water it is essential that the brakes be dried out before you press on. The simplest way is to drive for a hundred metres or so in low or second gear with your left foot on the brake pedal. Even when you've done this, check them to make sure you have full braking power before resuming normal touring speed.

And that's that. One final word of warning. Don't ever treat water too lightly. More crashes occur on wet roads than are proportional to the degree of difficulty. People just don't realize how much care they should take.

SNOW

As with water, there are varying degrees of snow, and equally obviously there are some levels of snow through which it is impossible to drive anything. You should never be trying to drive through snow on other than made roads. This point, in fact, raises the first difficulty. It is quite often almost impossible to determine where the road goes. In some cases this won't be a major problem because you'll be driving through a drift of, say 30 to 40 metres, and you'll be able to see where the road emerges at the other end of the drift. However, there could be times where your only guide is a line of trees or embankments. Unless you are absolutely *sure* where you are going to drive, don't drive at all.

Then of course there are different forms of snow. Hardpacked snow is really more like driving on ice; melting slushy snow is rather similar to driving in water; softer snow covering on a hard road base is a different story altogether. For this you will almost certainly need chains, which quite literally wrap around the tyre/wheel assembly and provide traction. At the very least you will need good quality mud and snow tyres. Most commonly you will have variations of surface through all three types of snow covering.

The secret of making satisfactory progress under such conditions is to keep the vehicle moving. Again, avoiding any violent or even sudden use of brakes, power or steering and selecting the highest gear you can get away with, you simply move steadily forward, checking any slide before it gets out of hand and slipping the clutch occasionally to keep the engine spinning freely. (For this reason in fact manual cars are easier to drive in snow than automatics and specially so if you are skilful with your use of gearbox and clutch.) If the car stops there is a reasonable chance that it will not go again because you will get nothing but wheelspin and will eventually bog down. If it goes too fast you will have trouble controlling the slides which must occur and it will be difficult to check the speed without locking up the wheels.

Again one very strong final warning. Do not, *ever*, drive on a lonely road that you don't know in heavy snow. Be specific about your destination; know how far it is and preferably check road conditions even for that road with the relevant authorities before you set out.

ICE

Bearing in mind that hardpacked snow virtually becomes ice, the system of driving applies pretty much as it does in the previous section. However, there is another form of ice which need not necessarily be associated in any way with snow conditions. In very cold weather it is possible for a road surface to freeze over in sections because of excessive frost or because water from poor road drainage has frozen on the surface. Snow is obvious. You can see it and there is usually plenty of warning. Ice is much more sneaky. You can drive for hours on a winter's night on a road which is both dry and fast and then very suddenly come across a patch of ice, perhaps not more than 10 metres wide. That's just enough to send you sliding off into the bushes. Take special care going into blind corners and over crests: anywhere, in fact, where you can't see ahead. If it is a very cold night and you are driving on a road which has no signpost indication of its potential condition, be alert and aware enough to recognize the possibility. Slow down and take the above precautions.

If it is a very cold night and you are driving on a road which has no signpost indication of its potential condition, be alert and aware enough to recognize the possibility. Slow down and take the above precautions.

If you do come across ice unexpectedly it is a certainty that you are going to slide. As it happens, ice patches are not usually very lengthy and the chances are that the car will be off the ice before the slide has reached really dangerous proportions. However, don't just sit there hoping. Feel and be aware of the degree and direction of the slide, and correct for it so that when you come back on to a good surface again you can quickly bring the car back to its correct tracking situation.

Under most conditions for most drivers, ice presents the greatest hazard of all. It provides absolutely no adhesion. Therefore you can reasonably assume that if you hit a large patch of unexpected ice you will go out of control. If you go out of control slowly, even a crash has the potential to be a minor one. If you continue to drive fast on roads where ice is a possibility, your crash will be a hum-dinger.

DIRT AND/OR MUD

Driving on dirt can be a lot of fun. If it wasn't, there would be no rallies and no rally drivers. It is, under controlled conditions, an excellent way to learn more about car control and specially about mastering slides. However, it can also be hazardous for those who are not used to it and who don't take the necessary care. Dirt roads have more adhesion capability than water, snow or ice, but less than bitumen. Smooth dirt is almost no problem at all if you simply slow down a little and again concentrate on being as smooth as possible. Almost always, however, dirt roads have bumps, potholes and corrugations and each and all of these tend to upset the balance and stability of the car and increase the degree of hazard.

Humps. Brake on approach

Accelerate on the rise

Brake on the crest

Dips. Brake into dip

Accelerate out

Potholes

The first thing to remember about potholes is that they can not only present a danger but also be suspension breakers. Your ability to read the road will help here. Crashing into a sudden deep hole in the road can cause a loss of control; it can also smash the front end out of the car and leave you stranded. So it is very important to concentrate hard on the road ahead. Unless you are a dirt road specialist, it is a good idea to drive slowly over badly broken roads. You cannot swerve suddenly to miss a hole because this will throw the car into a violent slide from which you may not be able to recover. For this reason it is sometimes better to drive through a hole than try to avoid it. If the potholes are small and there are a lot of them, it is possible to get the car to such a speed that it will skip over most of them; but you still have to slow down for the curves, otherwise you will have the combination of loss of adhesion plus a bouncing suspension to cope with.

Play it by ear. The general rule is that it is better to slow down and arrive with an undamaged car than press on and stand the chance of breaking both the car and yourself.

Corrugations

Sometimes, and specially on corners where the road is slightly banked, water running across the road will have caused corrugations. Usually these miniature humps and dips will be consistent in wave length. It is also very likely that you will come across such corrugations unexpectedly as you enter a turn on a reasonably smooth dirt road. The corrugations will set up a harmonic sequence of motion in the suspension, especially in the rear and more particularly if the car has a live axle suspension set up. As a result, the wheels will now spend not more than half their time actually touching the road. When they do touch, it will be violently, and what they will be touching is poorly adhesive dirt. What chance now of stopping the back end from sliding? Be warned! The resultant slide can be vicious and, simply because of the continuing undulations in the road surface, it's also possible for the (now sideways) rear wheel to dig into the dirt and flip the car into a roll.

It helps, of course, to know of the possibilities. Again, read the road. And where you can't see, slow down until you are sure of what you're driving into.

Dips and humps

Often on dirt roads, and sometimes also on bitumen, you come across dips and humps or crests. They're no problem if you know they exist. But come across either unexpectedly while you are travelling even moderately fast, and you'll know all about it. You stand a fair chance of smashing the suspension in the bottom of the dip, or of getting airborne and then smashing the suspension on the landing after the hump.

For those drivers who have mastered left-foot braking in automatics, here's a chance to really exploit the technique. Manual drivers simply need some deft footwork. On approaching and recognizing the existence of a dip in the road, brake firmly and smoothly and continue to brake over the lip. Lift off the brake and sharply re-apply power just as you reach the bottom of the dip. This serves the purpose of lifting the nose of the car and extending the travel of the suspension so that there is less chance of 'bottoming out' (the process of reaching the full bump position of the suspension). Once the car clears the exit lip, ease back on the accelerator and resettle at the cruising speed.

The process for humps and crests is similar. If there is a sharp rise off a flat approach, brake on the approach and then sharply accelerate at the beginning of the rise to lift the front of the car. Right on the crest, brake again lightly to drop the nose and reduce the chance of flying. It is important to try to cross humps and crests square on. Then if the car does fly you can be reasonably sure it will land squarely. If it lands with any degree of sideways attitude to the road, the tyres will slide momentarily and you will need to correct as for any other type of skid or slide.

Using the left foot technique for automatics saves time in the various changes from brake to power and back again, but it needs practice. Actually it is surprising just how much one can smooth out the nastiest of dips and humps just by following the above procedure.

All of the things we've just talked about can and will present difficulties from time to time. Probably the biggest problem of all is that each or any of these conditions occurs only occasionally and for that reason one does not get enough chance to practise the required techniques and become proficient at them. Still, it is an advantage, at least, to know how. If and when you are taking a trip in which any of the above may be encountered, it might be as well to re-read this section and then try to get some practice. If that's not on, then take it all very carefully until you begin to understand and can accurately interpret what's happening with the car.

TOWING A CARAVAN OR TRAILER

In most countries of the world it is not necessary to hold a special licence or even have any sort of licence endorsement to tow a large trailer or caravan. Yet to be able to drive a semi-articulated truck one needs some specialized training and a special licence test. The implication is that driving a car with a trailer attached is easier and less dangerous, which is simply not true.

Small box-type trailers are not particularly difficult to drive and neither, in fact, are larger trailers provided they are low sided with a centre of gravity which is close to the ground. But high sided trailers and caravans are a different story altogether, as many a novice operator has found out to his everlasting sadness.

The real dangers lie in the mechanics of the hitch, the climatic influences of wind and rain, and the design and condition of the road. All three are worth considering, both separately and collectively, but as a starter the object of the exercise is to try to remove any influence which causes snaking and/or swaying. Unfortunately, a trailer and its towing vehicle constitute a mechanical

system that has a number of degrees of freedom of movement. The exercise is to try to keep all of these in check.

It is first necessary to consider the weight and size of both the towing vehicle and that which is to be towed. There is almost never any problem when the towing vehicle is substantially larger than the towed, as would be the case, for example, if a truck were pulling a small box trailer. However, when it is required that the family car pull a holiday caravan a different set of circumstances arises and the size of the trailer will be determined by the size and weight of the car. As a general rule of thumb, the trailer should be at least lighter than the car. In some cases local laws demand this anyway. It is possible, with some modern trailer hitches, to break this rule of thumb but it requires expert advice and guidance and, usually, a fair amount of expense on the hitching devices. When building, buying or renting a trailer it is also necessary to keep in mind such design features as location of axle or axles and the suspension and braking systems used. Ideally the axle should be somewhat to the rear of a point midway between the tow point and rear of the trailer. If it is a large trailer it may well be desirable (if not essential in some cases) to have a tandem axle arrangement the better to spread the weight of the trailer. The suspension will almost always be by semi-elliptic leaf springs but good quality hydraulic dampers should be used as well. There are three choices of braking systems—mechanical, hydraulic and electrical, and again these may be operated by vacuum, electrical impulse or simply mechanical over-ride in almost any combination. It is impossible to describe the best system here because of the potential variations of both trailer design and usage. However, just having that knowledge implies that you should consult a recognized expert in the field before making any decisions about which composite system you will use.

Tyres and tyre pressures are perhaps even more critical on a trailer than they are on a car which is at least directly controllable by the driver. It is generally considered that cross ply tyres are more suitable for trailer use than radials, since the factor of the tyre rolling about on the rim contributes to trailer instability. From my own experience, however, radial tyres are entirely suitable provided that the pressures are kept well up. How far up depends on the laden weight of the trailer, but certainly not less than 35 psi. Even with cross ply tyres it is necessary to run fairly high pressures (around the 30 psi for example). The high pressure increases the stability of the tyre.

Another factor of trailer stability is the location of any load being carried within the trailer. This should be located as near as possible to the centre of gravity of the whole trailer and spread evenly across the trailer floor in this area.

Finally, the trailer hitch itself has to be considered. There are far too many badly designed towbars about and, in most countries, no standards by which one can be guided at the time of purchase.

It is true as a generalization that almost any reasonably located towbar will work if all it is required to carry is a small domestic or commercial trailer. However, simply having a cheap towbar fitted to your car tends to be an encouragement to use it for bigger and better things occasionally, and for this reason alone it is worth buying a good quality bar in the first place. At least two of the towbar mounting points should project well forward of the most rearward point of the towing vehicle, usually somewhere in the vicinity of the differential housing on a rear wheel drive car. Since a good sized trailer with its axle mounted slightly aft of its lateral centrepoint will be throwing a good deal of its weight forward on to the towing point (the tow ball), two further matters need to be considered. First, the towbar and ball will need to be strong enough to accept that weight, not just statically but also under all conditions encountered while the combination is in motion.

Second, such weight will tend to depress the rear springs of the car and consequently raise the front, thus reducing the steering capacity of the car (since the front tyres now have less effective contact with the road). For this reason some sort of load levelling levers should be used. Usually these will connect to the vehicle towbar and run back along the 'A' frame of the trailer towing coupling, where they will be held in place under tension to help raise the back of the car to somewhere near normal ride height. If the load levellers are of the latest modern design they will also have a cam arrangement at the point where they connect to the frame of the trailer coupling and will be free to move slightly fore and aft while the combination is in motion. Should the trailer begin any process sway, the levelling lever will ride up on the cam, helping to control any potential sway.

If all of these precautions are taken there will be very little chance of the trailer adopting any snaking or swaying characteristics, particularly if the driver then adopts certain special driving habits as well. Most importantly, speed is a contributing factor to trailer stability. Quite simply, there are speeds at which almost all trailers can begin to become unstable. These speeds vary from trailer to trailer, but usually 50 mph is fast enough for all combinations and is the statuary limit in the UK. Trailers can be affected by road conditions such as severe camber or rough broken edges and the driver should be alert to such conditions.

The skill of the driver will also be an influencing factor and again smoothness of control is the over-riding technique. Sharp braking and/or steering can certainly upset the stability of a trailer and should be avoided (which of course means even greater concentration and anticipation to avoid situations which might cause such driving).

Wet or slippery roads will call for an extra degree of caution simply because the driver has at least one more set of wheels to control. And these are semi-detached from the car and therefore more difficult to control. High crosswinds are also a danger, particularly when one comes upon such conditions unexpectedly. The slab side of a high caravan makes a fine target for a sudden gust of wind and the driver will feel immediately the tendency for the wind to push the trailer about on its towing point, at the same time causing it to sway.

Ideally, in any situation where a trailer is either snaking or swaying (or both together), the driver should accelerate briefly to pull the whole rig straight. But unfortunately that's not always possible. One cannot accelerate into an area of potential danger. Therefore, again, it is necessary to generalize. If you do appear to be in a degree of trouble with an unstable trailer, slow down—gradually and carefully if possible, certainly never suddenly. Use the brakes only if necessary and as lightly as you can get away with.

Actually, a well set up, properly balanced trailer, carefully matched to its towing vehicle, is very rarely a problem even for an inexperienced driver. Most problems seem to occur because the rig was not well selected or engineered in the first place. If there seems to be a degree of inherent instability in any trailer you are required to drive, chances are you'll become aware of it quite quickly. You would be well advised to investigate and remedy the cause before proceeding further. If you are buying a trailer of any sort, it's as well to try to arrange a test tow before you make your final decision. The same applies if you are renting or borrowing.

The time and trouble taken will be well worth it in the long run.

Modifying your Car

MODIFYING YOUR CAR

1. Unmodified
2. Modified wheels and tyres only—and tyres are too 'fat'
3. Modified by lowering only
4. Lowered, and wheels and tyres again too 'fat'

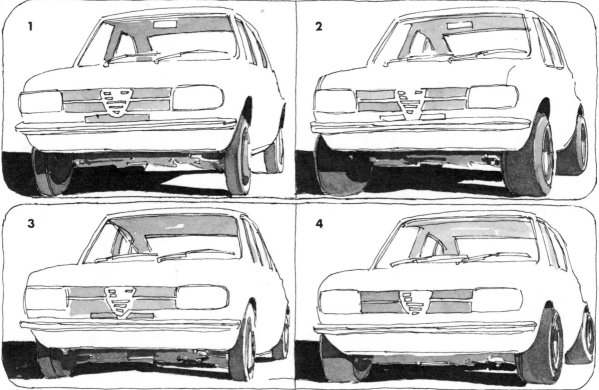

1. Wrong

There seems to be in this day and age, particularly with the younger driver, a great desire to change the car in some way from its original specifications. Certainly there is no reason why this should be disallowed, specially since modifications to a car can improve its overall performance. Unfortunately, however, far too many people carry out ill-advised modifications, which enhance the appearance of the car in some cases, but detract from its overall performance.

Basically there are two departments in which a car can be changed from standard. They are power and handling. Before you do anything, however, it would be as well to check with your local authority. Some modifications are banned by law to ensure that cars continue to comply with the appropriate design regulations.

It is possible to improve the handling of a car without modifying the available power. But it is highly inadvisable to increase the power without also doing something about the handling. So, since handling becomes the most important of the two, let's look at this department first.

HANDLING AND STEERING

The handling of a car is the manner in which it will go around a corner: its steerability and its stickability (a combination of body roll and adhesion).

The easiest and least expensive way to improve the handling and steering of a car is to pump the tyres harder. Simple as that. But there is a whole chapter on tyres and tyre pressures coming up next, so for our immediate purposes let's consider mechanical modifications and leave the tyres until later.

The introduction of wide wheels over the past ten years has provided an excellent opportunity for the young motorist to improve both the appearance and the handling of his car at relatively low cost. But in many cases the wide wheels modification has been carried to extremes and, as a result, legislation has been brought down to limit the wheel size to something reasonable. The wide wheels can cause problems for these reasons.

A car, as it comes from the manufacturer, has what I call roll/slip factor built into it. The standard wheels and tyres are wide enough to provide reasonable traction under normal circumstances. If the car is pushed beyond reasonable limits the tyres will lose their adhesion and the car will slide. A safety factor, believe it or not, because if it would not slide it would roll. Changing the tyres for a type which give better adhesion brings the slip factor down a little but not so much as to greatly influence the roll factor. The fitting of wheels not more than 3 centimetres wider than the standard wheels has a similar effect, even greater with wider, better tyres.

2. Right

Beyond this, however, the situation can become dangerous. Too much grip is now provided by the wheel/tyre combination and the car may roll before it slides. Certainly the cornering capacity of the car has improved but the ultimate result of overdoing it is much more disastrous. Besides, the body roll of the car has been increased to the point where it is less comfortable to ride in.

Other popular methods of effecting handling modifications are by lowering the car and fitting stiffer suspension. If the car is lowered and the suspension not stiffened nor the wheels changed there is a chance under severe cornering that the suspension will 'bottom'. When this happens the springs and/or shock absorbers reach the limit of their travel and the sudden loss of suspension movement will cause an equally sudden and unexpected slide—one which will be hard to control.

On the other hand, if the car is lowered and the wheels widened but the suspension otherwise left standard, then there is a reasonable chance that the wheels will rub on the springs or the guards when the car is cornered hard. This will increase the chances of a blow-out.

If the car is lowered and the springs and/or shock absorbers exchanged for stiffer units but the wheels and tyres left unchanged, the slip factor will be increased to a dangerous level and the car will want to slide about on every corner.

To bring about the improvement that most drivers are looking for, a little of all three modifications should be carried out. For example: wheels widened by 3 centimetres (and the tyres replaced with ones suited to the new rim size); body lowered on to suspension to a maximum of 3 centimetres provided no fouling will occur; and stronger double-acting shock absorbers fitted. In most cases, however, the costs of such modifications are prohibitive for the average driver, so he does one or the other and the end result is a car which does not handle as well as when it left the production line.

A popular method of modifying handling characteristics is to fit a proprietary anti-roll bar of some kind. Generally a driver decides he does not specially like the natural understeer characteristics of his car and so he fits an anti-roll bar to the rear. The result is a stiffer rear end which will not stick to the road as well. In other words, rather than cure the understeer, he simple builds in oversteer. In my opinion that's wrong. The general rule is that if you have a problem at the front (understeer) you cure it at the front; if you have a problem at the back (oversteer) you cure it at the back. Again generalizing, the basic road car should be stiffer at the front than at the back. This will give steering accuracy and adhesion, always provided that the front is not excessively stiff. Remember that body roll at least to some extent helps to dissipate cornering forces; to remove it may well produce flatter cornering but it also places

73

a much greater stress on the tyres which, if they are not both wider and of better rubber compound, will now slip more easily.

What it all means is that you must be careful of anti-roll bar fitting. Better to do the job with shock absorbers, wheels and tyres. Or alternatively, get truly expert advice. And be careful about who you think to be an 'expert'.

Before leaving the subject of wide wheels there is another point which should be considered. The suspension of a car is designed to carry a certain amount of upsprung weight. The widening of a set of standard steel wheels imposes on that suspension more strain than it was originally intended to carry, with corresponding increases in wear on spring mountings, wheel bearings and so on. If a set of wider wheels is contemplated it is advisable to wait until you can afford a set of good quality lightweight wheels such as those cast from various alloys of magnesium or aluminium. As it happens they are also considerably stronger than steel wheels.

MODIFYING THE ENGINE

We have already established that the engine should not be modified to give more power until the handling has been improved to cope with it. Even then, when engine changes are contemplated, the foremost consideration must be that the car is still for ordinary road use. For this reason the extreme high performance modifications available for racing are impractical for road use.

Such things as extractor exhaust systems (provided they are adequately muffled), a mildly reground camshaft, multiple carburettors and a gentle polish of the internal surfaces of the cylinder head are acceptable, even desirable, if they are done properly and with economical operation in mind. However, the wild semi-racing cam, fat unmuffled exhausts, maximum porting and polishing; are all out so far as I am concerned, because they are breaking the laws in some cases and also they are boorish and impractical. A modification to a car which has no practical or economic value has obviously been done for some other purpose, that purpose usually being to show off. And this sort of thing is for immature, baby-brained people who should not have driving licences.

The thing that most surprises me about modifications to both handling and suspension is that when the job is well done it is usually also expensively done. For an equivalent amount of money the modifier would probably have bought a car with a higher performance potential to begin with. Then all the changes would have been unnecessary. Which brings up another point.

BUYING YOUR CAR

When you are shopping for a car, consider well the amount of money you have to spend and the purpose to which you wish to put the car. Don't take the first offer that comes your way because the salesman is prepared to give you an extra £50 on your trade. That £50 and a good deal more might go down the drain chasing away the frustration of an underpowered, impractical car.

Once you've made the decision to buy a new car (and it doesn't matter much whether it's actually new or second hand, it's still new to you), carefully consider the following information. In fact, make out a detailed check list and then methodically work through. In the long run it will be well worth the effort.

THE CAR BUYERS' SELECTION GUIDE

Take out a large piece of paper and go to work. At the top of the page write down the absolute maximum price you can afford to pay (and be realistic about it). Next make a list of the cars you would like to own (but ensuring that none of them exceeds the maximum budget or you'll be defeating your purpose before you even begin). Now consider the following and make notes on each car. These are the things people want—and that means everybody.

safety: What sort of image does each car have in this regard? Do you know of any special problems with regard to both primary and secondary safety?

performance: Think of performance in the overall sense. That is, braking, steering, handling, ride, engine, fuel consumption, and so on. Do you know of any single undesirable feature?

appearance: Up to you, of course, but is it functional? The shape can have an effect on your ability to park it, for example, and may also influence its road performance through aerodynamics.

comfort: Much more important than most people realize. Is there sufficient seat adjustment? Does the seat hold you firmly in place? Does it give support in the right places—under the thighs, in the small of the back, around the shoulders? Do you sit on the seat or in the seat? What about access? Passengers reasonably catered for? Are the steering wheel and pedals located correctly for your shape and size?

economy: Again fuel consumption, but a lot more too. Try to establish the resale value at about the time/age you might want to sell it. Do you have or can you get any information about the cost of parts and servicing? Allowing for the replacement of common items, such as brake linings, spark plugs, tyres, exhaust systems, can you afford to run it? Will the depreciation leave you out of pocket when you want to replace it?

durability: There's an overlap here with economy but you will need to consider at what point of time might a car be, mechanically, at the end of the road (if you'll excuse the pun). As well, there is the possibility that the car of your choice might spend as much time in the workshop as it does on the road.

When you have done with all those points, do you have any specific personal requirements of a car? Run through the things you know that you will expect of your car, such as:

I do lots of country driving/ I do no country driving.

I carry two adults and two children most of the time/ I carry myself and one other most of the time.

I want two doors/ I want four doors.

I will carry a lot of luggage/ I never carry anything more than a few parcels.

I want to tow a boat or caravan/ I do not need lots of power.

There are obviously many more things which only you will know about. The point of all this, of course, is that by following the above method the chances of your forgetting something important are reduced. It's a bit late, three weeks after you've bought the car, to discover that it fails to do the job you want it to do in even one department, let alone two or three.

Finally you should be able to narrow your selection down to three cars at the most. When you reach this stage, go out and begin your wheeling and dealing. Chances are you will really like what you get and that alone will make you a better driver.

Tyres and Tyre Pressure

10

TYRES AND TYRE PRESSURE

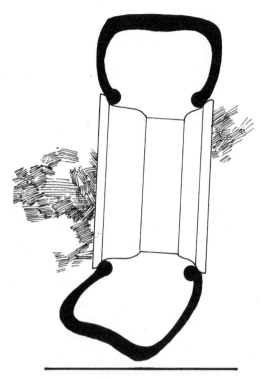

1. The cross ply tyre distorts in such a way as to remove the tread contact patch to the sidewall

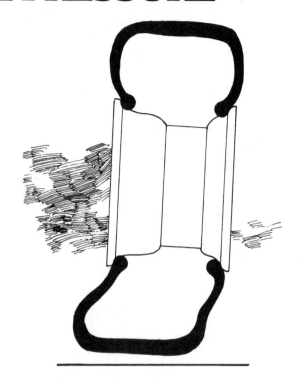

2. The radial flexes somewhat differently, maintaining at least to some degree a tread rubber contact with the road

In this fabulous day and age you can buy a tyre for every day of the week. Which of course is silly, but wouldn't it be beautiful to be able to do it? To have a full set of tyres in your garage for every purpose—a set for the rain, a set for the hot-dry, a set for the cold-dry, a set for town, a set for country. In fact, therein lies your whole tyre problem. When you buy tyres you have to find one set which will do all that, and more probably.

There's a wealth of extraordinarily good tyres on the market today. But there is also considerable confusion resulting from such supply. There are cross ply tyres, radial tyres, bias-belted tyres, nylon tyres, rayon tyres, fibreglass tyres and steel-belted tyres; and standard profile tyres and low profile tyres. There are tyres with numbers and letters such as 185/70xHR13, 165SR13 and 6.40x13.

So what do you do? You rely on your tyre supplier to advise you and he puts you on tyres which have the highest profit margin—or stock he's trying to get rid of. Mainly because he doesn't know much better than you. And I don't mean that disrespectfully. Most tyre dealers carry only one brand and they know very little about other brands which might be better for your purposes. So I first have to agree that it is very difficult for you to decide which tyres *you* should buy. But the following might be of help.

Right from the outset I am excluding all retreads from any consideration. I have not yet seen a retread I could trust under all conditions—and you can't drive only on dry days and only on smooth roads, and always at a maximum of 45 mph. Besides, you can't economize at the cost of your life.

The first choice to arise therefore is between conven-

tional and radial ply. In broad terms, radial tyres give longer life and a greater degree of cornering stability than cross ply tyres. They cost a little more, but generally will give better overall economy because of the extra life. Radial tyres have thinner sidewalls than cross ply tyres and are therefore more flexible. They should be run with a pressure approximately four pounds per square inch higher than a conventional tyre to overcome excessive flexibility and to remove a bagginess in the walls which makes them prone to stone and gutter fracture.

The disadvantages of radial tyres are mainly psychological. The extra cornering power offered by such tyres can induce people to drive faster than they should, providing new problems of car management. The limit of adhesion of the radial tyre is usually higher than that of the cross ply, which means that when the limit is reached the car is going faster. The subsequent loss of control will therefore be potentially more dangerous on radials than on cross plies.

On some cars radial tyres are not as effective as good quality cross ply tyres however, and some of the modern low profile, wide-section cross ply tyres are every bit as good as most radials, if yours is such a car. It should also be understood that if low profile tyres are fitted as a replacement for conventional profile tyres the overall gearing of the car will be lower, meaning that the engine will rev harder for less road speed in each gear. Low profile tyres are those marked with a 70 or 60 somewhere in the size designation, for example, 185/70xHR13. The 70 means that the depth of the tyre is 70 per cent of the width; it is wider than it is deep.

The next question you need to ask yourself is whether you want a tyre which will give its best performance in the dry or in the wet. Since most of your driving will be done in the dry it is reasonable to assume that you will prefer tyres which offer a high degree of dry weather road holding. The road holding ability of a tyre depends mainly upon its tread pattern and the compound of rubber used in its manufacture. Some tyres are designed in such a way that the tread pattern squishes water on the road out from under the tyre as it rolls along. Others have a tendency to trap the water beneath the tyre and to cause 'aquaplaning'—the tendency for the tyre to ride up on to the water and lose its grip on the road. Again, a tyre with a soft rubber compound generally gives a better degree of adhesion than one with a hard compound, the soft tyre being 'stickier'.

However, the soft tyre also wears out faster and what you gain in the wet you will almost certainly lose in economy. On today's market there are a number of all-weather tyres which have been designed for a variety of conditions which give good wet and dry road holding and quite long life.

You should decide now whether you want tubeless or tubed tyres. If your car is fitted with the late type safety rims then you should have no hesitation in asking for tubeless tyres. They are less prone to puncture and blow-out and, because there is no internal friction between tube and tyre wall, they do not build up in pressure on long trips the way that tubed tyres do. But if your car does not have safety rims I would strongly recommend that you use tubed tyres.

The only other point left for us to discuss is tyre size and pressures. In Chapter 9 on modifying your car, I mentioned that the simplest way to make your car handle better was to pump the tyres harder. I also went into some detail about modifying wheel sizes and the problems associated with this. Both topics come up again now since tyres and tyre pressures can have a significant effect on the handling of your car.

In general, the manufacturers of your car have fitted it with a wheel size which is best suited to the car's suspension and steering mechanisms. It is possible to go 3 centimetres wider than standard in wheel size without there being any detrimental effect, but you have to bear in mind that if you do this you will also have to buy a new set of tyres. The tyres you buy for your car at any time *must* fit the rims.

Obviously, I am not talking about putting a 14 inch tyre on a 13 inch rim. It just won't fit. But I am talking about the rim width. For example, it is possible to put a 185 radial tyre on a 4½ inch rim, but the tyre is so much too wide for the rim that it becomes dangerously unstable. You can also put a 155 radial on a 6 inch rim with equally disastrous results. To guide you in the selection of a tyre size for the rims of your car, I have included a chart which gives ideal tyre/wheel sizes.

It is generally known that when you intend to undertake a long trip and will be driving faster than your normal around-town speed you should increase the pressure in your tyres. What is generally *not* known is what pressures you should increase from. In other words, what should the normal pressures be? Unfortunately, your only guide to basic tyre pressures is the handbook for your car, put out by the manufacturer. In the interests of both comfort and basic safety, he recommends a pressure which is relatively low.

Up to a point, a car will hold the road better, the higher the pressure in the tyre. The reason for this is that at high pressures the tyre does not distort as much on the trim, ensuring that the tread, or part of it, remains in contact with the road. On low pressures under hard cornering the tyre is inclined to roll under the rim, running mostly on the side wall as it does. Not only does this reduce adhesion; it also increases the possibility that the tyre will pull away from the rim to the point where the edge of the rim digs into the ground and trips the car, which may ultimately roll over.

Certainly the low pressures are more comfortable. As well, low pressures will induce possible loss of traction at reasonably low speeds so that if you are pushing too hard the resultant slide will be easier to control than one which occurs at high speed. But personally, I would rather have maximum adhesion at all times and then make sure I drive within the cornering limits of that adhesion. For this reason, I advocate higher pressures than those usually found in the maker's handbook.

The ratio between front and rear pressures is the next important consideration. Since we have established that the tyres will grip better as the pressure increases, we can now consider where we require the best grip. In a car which understeers, that is, slips at the front, we would obviously need to have the pressures slightly higher at the front than at the rear. And vice versa. While if we have a car which tends to initial understeer and final oversteer we could set the pressures the same front and rear.

What it all boils down to is this. For a car which understeers on cross ply tyres, the pressures should be set at about 28 psi in the front and 26 psi in the rear. On radials the same pressures would be 32 front and 30 rear. A front wheel drive which understeers and which also has all its weight up front should be set at about 28/24 for cross plies and 32/28 for radials. A rear wheel drive car which oversteers and has all its weight at the back should be set at about 24/28 for cross plies and 28/32 for radials. These pressures are guidelines only and can certainly be adjusted slightly up or down as suits your personal taste. But they should not be far off those I have laid down.

In motor sport events it is not uncommon to get pressures as high as 40 psi or greater but such pressures are only effective on very smooth surfaces. On the road such pressures would not only be disastrously uncomfortable; they would also cause the tyre to bounce on any bump or ripple and a loss of adhesion would result (for an entirely new reason, that the tyre is now spending a good deal of its life in the air).

Often when you buy a new car it is a worthwhile investment either to insist that it is fitted with the tyres of your choice before you take delivery, or to swap the tyres for something a little better yourself as soon after you take delivery as possible. As I have said before, tyres are an inexpensive and very effective way of ensuring that your car is as safe on the road as you can reasonably make it.

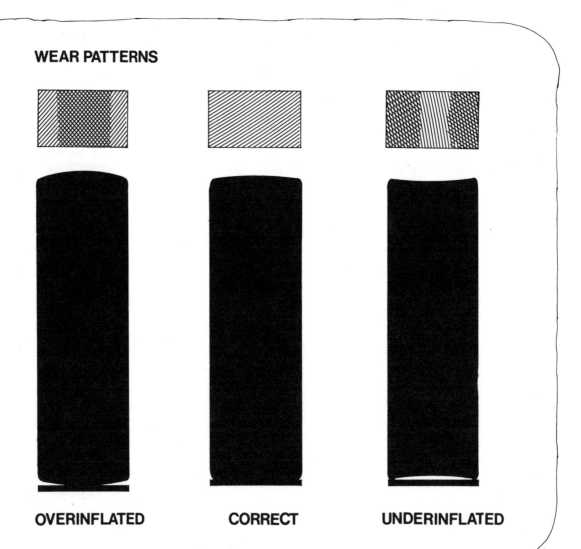

WEAR PATTERNS

OVERINFLATED   CORRECT   UNDERINFLATED

TYRE WIDTH/RIM WIDTH RATIO

RADIAL SIZE	CROSS PLY SIZE	RIM WIDTH (inches)
145	5.20/5.50	4½
155	5.60/5.90	5
165	6.40/6.50/6.00/6.45	5½
175/185	6.70/7.10/7.00	6
185/195	7.35/7.50/7.60/7.75	6½
205/215	8.15/8.25/8.45/8.55	7
225/234	8.85/9.15	7½

There is a degree of flexibility in this chart to the extent that it is entirely reasonable to overlap one tyre size either way. A 5 inch rim will take a 145, 155 or 165 radial tyre without problems. A 6 inch rim will take 175 or 185 and perhaps even 195. Liberties with tyre/rim combinations should not be taken beyond this margin.

The Law and You

11

THE LAW AND YOU

Even before you manage to get your driving licence, you will have come into contact with the law as it applies to the motorist. As a pedestrian you will be aware that the law provides you with right of way over the car on a marked foot crossing. When you first make application for a permit to learn to drive you will be given a copy of the Highway Code which contains most of the laws which will affect you as a motorist and you will be required to learn them. If you are like most motorists you will skimp on these and learn only those which you think the testing officer will be likely to ask you when you take your driving test.

Even with such a brief knowledge of the laws which apply to driving you will possibly be able to drive for years without being convicted of anything more than a parking offence. This does not make you a good driver—any more than having a thorough knowledge of the laws makes you a good driver. But obviously you will be a better driver if you *do* know the law.

Unfortunately, knowing the law will not stop you being killed or killing someone else. Even abiding by the law does not always help in this regard. Which is a good reason why the extreme punitive measures taken against motorists by most governmental authorities have not been sufficiently effective in curbing the road toll.

The laws as they apply to motorists are made to protect your fellow drivers from you—and you from them. Some are designed to protect you from yourself. Yet again, certain motoring laws are made to provide convenience.

Breaking the laws of motoring renders you liable to fines, imprisonment, or suspension or cancellation of your driving licence. And yet, some laws of motoring need to be broken from time to time to ensure a smooth flow of traffic. Incongruous maybe, but true.

On metropolitan roads where the speed limit is generally about 30 mph, at certain times and under certain conditions driving at 30 mph can be as dangerous as driving at 50 mph.

The law, as it happens, is not flexible on this point. If you are stopped by a police officer under such conditions you will still be regarded as having broken the law. With such inflexibility there are problems. It is abundantly clear to the average motorist that the police are out to get convictions, to bring in revenue—to fight fire with fire as it were. It is a great pity that the instructions to the police do not include, or at least make provision for, advice for the erring motorist. In certain instances a more lenient attitude might be more likely to beget results than the current hardline attitude. Unfortunately, however, there are still the 'criminal' motorists who laugh at lenience and exploit it as weakness, to make the lot of the average law-abiding driver even more hazardous.

It is obviously important for every motorist to know his rights under the law and to act upon them. I would not like to suggest that there are ways and means for a driver who is guilty of a blatant breach of the law to get away with it: it would be irresponsible to do so. However, there are certainly times and conditions under which a motorist is wrongly charged and he should know where he stands.

By way of an example, let me cite the following case. A driver was charged with culpable driving following a collision which resulted in the death of a passenger in the other car. The driver had lost control of his car on a slightly wet road while cornering at 50 mph, a speed which was just on the speed limit for the area. His was a quality car, fitted with good tyres and in excellent condition throughout. He was a driver of some fifteen years experience. Despite this however, he had never been in a slide or skid in any car, and when his car appeared to slide on this corner he panicked. He over-reacted to the slide and crashed into an oncoming vehicle. It was the sort of situation which could happen to any of us. The police considered that the driver was driving culpably because he allowed his car to get into such a slide on a public road where conditions were obviously not good enough for 50 mph speeds.

In his defence, the following points were brought up.
1. He had never been taught how to react to a slide of any sort—so he had no way of knowing what he should do to control the car once it did slide.
2. His car, with the tyres fitted to it, was potentially capable of taking any corner of similar radius to that on which the collision occurred at a speed of 50 mph without mishap on a wet or dry road, provided there were not other factors which could have influenced the handling of the car.
3. Other factors, however, could have been present and, from an examination of the section of road concerned, almost certainly were. The corner had a slight uphill gradient. On that corner it was found that diesel truck drivers had to accelerate hard to make the grade and that in doing so, a considerable amount of unburnt diesel fuel was deposited on the road surface. There it lay, settling into the bitumen until the first shower of rain floated the oily fluid to the surface, making that corner unnaturally slippery, more so in fact than most of the corners on the road before and after that point. The driver had arrived at the corner less than five minutes after the rain had started. The diesel fuel could therefore very easily have been the cause of the slide and it would not have required an excessive speed. Once the car was sliding, the untrained, unskilled driver tried to take some corrective action, but he simply over-reacted to the situation and put the car headlong into the lane of the other vehicle.

His driving, were these points all true, could hardly be described as culpable. He was simply an unskilled driver.

In closing the subject, let me say this. The laws of motoring are also the laws of common sense, with a few specifics thrown in. For the well-being of yourself and your fellow motorists, they must be obeyed as closely as possible—always provided that in doing so you are not inconveniencing and disrupting all the other traffic in your immediate vicinity. You will break the law quite regularly in one way or another when you are driving—everybody does. When you do, just make absolutely sure you are not breaking a law which will mean danger for others—and be prepared for the consequences.

Driving for Economy

12

DRIVING FOR ECONOMY

In the past few years motoring economy has become a significant factor in people's lives, for the first time since The Depression of the thirties. Never before have costs escalated as fast or to such an extent with everything from the cost of the car itself to the service of it and the fuel to keep it mobile going up faster than one can keep pace. As a result there are reasons now in existence for keeping motoring costs down which in the past have been relatively insignificant factors.

Even now it remains fixed in people's minds that there is not much they can do about it; that if you want to drive a car you have to accept the burden of rising costs. But, in fact, that is not entirely true. One of the problems of that sort of defeatist philosophy is that it tends to reduce the private car to the status of ordinary public transport. People view the car as a necessity; wholly as a means of transport. Rising costs have taken much, if not all, of the pleasure out of motoring. In a classic dog chasing its tail situation that attitude in turn means that drivers become less enthusiastic about and less interested in motoring than before, with the result that they are less efficient and dedicated drivers at a time when the precise opposite should be true.

If ever there was a time in the history of private motoring when the driver should be efficient, dedicated and alert it is now. Such an attitude can ensure the interested driver of two things: a better chance of avoiding potential collision situations (as has always been the case) AND substantially reduced motoring costs (which has also always been the case; but never before considered important enough to worry about). Should you elect to adopt the latter attitude and take a serious interest in your driving not only can you make gains in terms of the preservation of life and limb, and not only will it cost you less to operate your car, but you will also find that driving can still be a pleasure when all about you are giving up in disgust. Here is how to do it.

In all the foregoing chapters which concern themselves with technique there has been an overriding philosophy which encourages the driver to take it easy. Not necessarily slowly, mind you, because if you always drive slowly you will not be an accomplished driver, and neither will you find the business challenging and interesting. Taking it easy is more a state of mind than a driving technique. It means to be able to find the right speed and the right degree of effort for the mix of car, road and conditions which apply at the time. The same philosophy applies when economy is the goal.

There are of course, economy driving specialists whose techniques differ greatly from those which apply to day to day motoring and which should not be adopted. In some cases such techniques include coasting down hills to avoid using petrol, at the risk not only of life and limb but also at the expense of brake pads, linings, steering and suspension components (as a result of the extra stresses imposed on these areas to compensate for the lack of assistance normally provided by the engine). Even in organised economy runs, where coasting is specifically prohibited, it is possible still to descend steep hills, even mountains, in top gear, thus effecting fuel economies but requiring a very high degree of expertise and some risk.

Despite their effectiveness in achieving a short term special purpose result, such techniques are definitely not recommended for normal day to day driving. Although one tends to think of the cost of petrol being the most significant factor in economical motoring, it is important and very beneficial to consider all areas in which costs can be reduced and as it happens, the system which applies to one will apply to all. That is, when you learn to use the least amount of fuel possible, you will also be conserving other areas as well; i.e. tyres will last longer, suspension components will not wear so rapidly, engine and transmission parts will give better life.

Conservation begins, like everything else, at the beginning. The first cold start of the day is where you start saving. It is usually necessary to start a cold engine with the choke. In many cars these days the choke is automatic, an idiotic device if ever there was one, but one which we are forced to accept. Whether the choke be manual or automatic its function is the same and that is to enrich the fuel/air mixture with a higher than normal proportion of petrol. Thus, leaving the choke in use for a longer than necessary period of time uses more fuel and this is specially so if you sit at a standstill waiting for the engine to warm up before driving off. As well, the excess fuel being fed into the combustion chambers is not all burned, some of it runs down the cylinder walls, diluting the engine lubricant, with the result that there is a fractionally higher wear rate in this area. Use only as much choke as is necessary for the engine to fire and drive off immediately, with the choke still in use but using gentle throttle openings so that the engine will not cough and stall while it is developing its heat. As soon as the engine will run without the choke, stop using it. The same applies to the automatic choke, except that the driver does not have any say in whether or not it will be used. However, drive off immediately the engine starts and within a mile or so there will be sufficient warmth in the engine for the choke to switch off.

Most people drive around in a rush, conditioned by a sense of false urgency and trying hard to make time everywhere they go. This technique is very expensive and the greater the rush the greater the expense. The most significant factor, however, is that one rarely achieves anything at all other than expense. Gentle acceleration from rest may well have everyone 'burning' you off at the lights but amazingly enough you almost always catch them again at the next stop.

On a long trip, it is possible that driving to save petrol will cost you time. No one can deny it. In other words averaging 60 mph, it will take you seven hours to drive 420 miles. Driving at 50 mph average the same journey will take nearly eight and a half hours. But that

10 mph reduction in speed will result in a petrol saving of around 20% and by no means could an average of 50 mph be called dawdling. The answer is, of course, to leave the additional hour available while you are planning the journey. Once again there are commensurate savings in wear and tear on components (not to mention the driver and passenger who should arrive less strained).

This method of driving is easy. Simply use the highest gears possible for all situations and when accelerating get into the highest gear as early as possible, provided that in doing so the engine is not overloaded. Brake early and gently, accelerate gently, watch the traffic flow and try to anticipate stops and starts. Try for a high degree of fluidity of motion; keep the car flowing along as smoothly and as consistently as possible. As soon as you begin to achieve results you will be able to set your own levels of performance and it will inevitably depend on the best combination of the driver/car team.

Which raises another point in the petrol/money saving category. The business of buying a car has already been covered, and assuming that the car selected is practical in every sense, including petrol economy, the new owner now has to learn to care for it. Although there are some obvious points of maintenance which will be covered in the owner's manual there are other little tricks that will also help in maintaining fuel economy.

For example: a sludgy engine oil will create unnecessary drag and friction within the engine. In many cases it may be worthwhile changing engine oil inside the period recommended by the makers to take advantage of the 'slipperiness' of the newer oil. On the same subject, a high grade 'expensive oil' will offer better friction resistant qualities than a 'cheaper' low grade oil.

Often during a brake adjustment the mechanic will leave the drum brakes set at a point where the linings are just touching the drums. This certainly provides a good pedal with little travel but it also means some friction build up in the brakes themselves and, some drag and increased rolling resistance, thus, higher fuel bills. It is often better to sacrifice a centimetre or so of brake travel in order to have brakes which do not cause unnecessary drag.

Much the same thing applies to wheel bearings. In some tapered adjustable wheel bearings, too much pressure is applied on the adjusting nut and, again, drag is created. The same problem can occur if the wheel bearings are not regularly serviced and the grease becomes contaminated with dirt or breaks down in composition.

Tyre pressure is also an influencing factor in rolling resistance. If the driver neglects to regularly check his car's tyre pressure then they slowly lose pressure and may also increase the drag and require a fraction more horse-power to move the car along. For reasons which have been explained in Chapter 10, it is usually better to run tyre pressure slightly too high than too low with the benefit that rolling resistance is decreased and fuel consumption reduced.

Then there are such minor factors as driving with the parking (emergency) brake partly on, or driving with the foot resting on the brake pedal. And last but not least, perhaps the most important factor of all in keeping fuel costs down, the tune of the engine. Today's engines are even more finicky to keep in tune than were the simpler, less complex engines of the past. This is mainly due to the requirements of certain governments that engines be as 'clean' as possible in terms of polluting the atmosphere. Thus, it is important that the engine be maintained in as near perfect tune as possible. This means more regular tune-ups and if this seems contradictory in that a tune-up may well eat into the money you have just saved by driving more carefully, it is also worth remembering that a regular tune-up should cost relatively little, simply because there will be little to adjust, whereas leaving the engine for a considerable time between tune-ups can mean a sequence of expensive adjustments.

Motor Sport for Everyone

13

MOTOR SPORT
FOR EVERYONE

For reasons as dissimilar as lack of desire or just plain lack of money, most drivers never take on any form of competitive motor sport. This is a pity because nothing improves a driver's skill and anticipation quite so effectively as competition in any form. And there is a wide variety of forms of motor sport, each with something to offer the interested driver and in most cases each providing a category or classification which will suit the individual driver's ambitions and budget.

THE CLUBS
All forms of motor sport are organized and administered by clubs: groups of people who have a common interest in some particular aspect of the sport. There are clubs for owners of a particular type of car (such as the Austin Healey Owners Club), others based on a particular type of competitive or non-competitive driving, and others based on geographical location. Whatever the reasons for their formation they all have similar goals and interests: motor sport, the development of driving skill and the understanding of the motor car, plus pleasant social interaction with people with similar interests.

All clubs come under the administrative jurisdiction of the Federation Internationale de l'Automobile, with authority delegated in each country to local controlling bodies such as the RAC. Thus people everywhere enjoy much the same sport in all its diversified branches.

FORMS OF THE SPORT
Pure motor racing is a very expensive sport and is therefore closed to all but the few who can afford the sort of money it requires. But other motor sports have developed through the years which can be enjoyed by the driver with nothing more at his disposal than the family hack.

Gymkhanas / Autotests
Usually a gymkhana takes the form of a series of specified driving tests over a set course marked with flags. The driver, competing against the clock, strives for the greatest degree of accuracy and the best time. Sometimes held on a sealed surface, but more usually on grass or dirt, they provide tremendous entertainment and probably the greatest single test of driving skill. A gymkhana driver would rarely exceed 20 mph at any time; he is concerned primarily with precision, accuracy and timing in his driving.

Sprints

A sprint is conducted on a closed, sealed, motor racing circuit, usually hired by a club for a day of sport. Cars complete a timed lap of the circuit individually, usually doing only one lap at a time, run against the clock. Here it is quite simply the quickest timed lap of the day that wins, but since there are obvious advantages for the powerful sports or racing car, the organizing club provides classes based upon engine size and type of car. So the man with the family hack has a chance to take out a trophy in his own class, and again precision, accuracy and an understanding of high speed vehicle control are essential for success.

In fact most competitors in sprints never win a trophy of any kind. But still they continue to compete. They become intent upon improving their own performances and thus are continuing to develop driving skills.

Rallies

Car rallies fall into two sharply defined areas—social and competitive. A social rally may take any of several forms—Treasure Hunt, Observation Rally, Photo Rally, Signpost Trial, and so on. All these simply involve a group of cars being driven from one point to another, with a navigator or observer finding the way and/or gathering the required information. There is no overall time for the journey, no intermediate control or check points and no penalty for late arrival.

A competitive rally is a very real test of driving and navigation skill. Such rallies are generally run over distances of from 200 to 600 miles, usually with the competitive stages at night through quiet country areas such as forestry roads. There is a control point at the end of each stage and drivers are allowed a prescribed time to complete their journey. Generally they are conducted on hard-to-find roads, and very often such roads are at least partially unmade. Route directions in a coded form are given to the navigator who is required to keep the driver on the right route at the correct average speed to complete the stage on time.

Rallies are inevitably gruelling, long distance events run over difficult terrain on unmade roads—hence the spectacular water splash
(Photo courtesy Racing Car News)

In rallycross each competitor is against the clock but the fact that he is in with other competitors encourages him to go faster

Hillclimbs

Hillclimbing has been a recognized form of motor sport for almost as long as racing itself and obviously it involves the negotiation of a hill in the shortest possible time. Usually such hills are sealed and therefore they resemble a section of conventional road. They are invariably steep over most of the course which can vary in length from 400 metres to 10 miles. Cars are started one at a time and again race against the clock. Such is the art and finesse required for championship hillclimbing that many drivers build special cars and compete in no other forms of the sport. Club hillclimbing, however, provides various classes so that once again it is possible to take part in the family car, as thousands do, and derive enjoyment and excitement from the challenge.

Trials

This sport requires a very special type of car built for this particular purpose and while the cars vary greatly they are basically the same in that they have little or no bodywork, high wheels, specially grooved tyres and room for a passenger whose energetic job it is to keep the weight over the back wheels to provide maximum traction. The course is always muddy and it is kept well watered during the event. Time is the enemy again, and skill and dexterity are the passwords to success.

Rallycross

Rallycross is a development of the rally designed to provide spectacle and entertainment for television and live audiences. A course similar to that for a rally special stage is built within an enclosed area as a circuit and the drivers compete to establish the quickest time on the circuit over a specified number of laps. The sport has gained tremendous popularity with TV audiences in England and Australia, mainly due to the fact that the circuit is designed with various surface changes and many humps and dips. It is quite spectacular to watch a fast car fly through the air for 10 metres or more over a hump and then see it plunge through a trough of water up to 40 centimetres deep and 3 metres in length. Again, however, it requires a special sort of car, and the costs of producing such a car are rapidly gaining on those required to build a competitive racing car. Not recommended for the family car!

A pretty little hillclimb special, built especially for the job of running short distances, up steep hills, very fast
(Photo courtesy Racing Car News)

Racing

When the money is available and the skill is sufficiently developed, this is the ultimate form of motor sport. For this reason we will dwell on the subject in more detail.

Before getting too deeply involved in the more formal aspects of race driving, let's discuss the philosophy of motor racing. Why do we go motor racing? How did it all start?

The best answer to this is also the most obvious. People go motor racing because they enjoy it, in the same way as people enjoy any other active and competitive sport. But there is in motor racing an element of risk and danger and challenge that is not present to quite the same extent in any other sport (except sky-diving which is also rather unusual). Motor racing began as a sport. It was a simple matter of one automobile manufacturer making the statement that his car could go faster, longer than anyone else's. The challenge was taken up as automatically as any other similar challenge would be and motor racing was born.

Since then motor racing has blossomed into the largest spectator sport in the world. And in the process it has made an invaluable contribution to the motor industry in so far as the development of the automobile is concerned. Dangerous—yes—but so are many other activities which have been of benefit to man and his scientific and industrial studies. However it remains primarily a sport and while people enjoy participating and watching and officiating it needs no further justification.

Now let's see what it is all about.

MOTOR RACING
Regulations
The regulations laid down for any type of motor sport are there for a very good purpose. They are designed specifically to protect the competitors, the organizers, the promoters, the administrators, the officials, and in fact everyone who is in any way connected with the sport. There are occasions when many of the regulations seem tedious and unnecessary but they have developed from many years of experience and all of them are important. It is the intending competitor's duty and responsibility to ensure that he is familiar with at least those which apply to him. The regulations which will apply most particularly are those relating to the modifications and alterations that can be made to a car. These will vary depending on the category of racing, but it is essential that they be understood and observed. Failure to comply with such regulations can, and usually does, mean cancellation of a driver's competition licence for a period. If the infringement was obviously intentional the period of cancellation can be as long as forever. So you can see how significant the regulations are.

Driver preparation
There are many points to be considered: the driver's mental attitude, his physical condition, his personal equipment, the safety and performance standards of his car. Since each point is as significant as the next we must consider them individually.

The mental attitude of a race driver will largely determine whether he is likely to be at all successful. For example, a race driver must be aggressive, but he should be completely in control of his aggression so that it does not become dangerous. He must be able to approach his sport realistically; it is a dangerous sport and any driver who fails to admit this and who has no fear will be a danger to himself and to others. His mental approach to the sport will probably also have a significant effect on his physical condition.

A race driver needs to be as physically fit as a participant in any other active sport; he should look after himself accordingly. Specifically, in the seven days immediately preceding a race meeting he should get plenty of sleep and should not drink alcohol. Apart from that, any normal routine form of exercise will suffice.

A driver's personal equipment consists of gear which will assist him to drive safely and at the same time provide some protection in the case of an accident. Any racing driver, regardless of the type of car or the class in which he races, must provide himself with the maximum protection. He *must* wear fire-proof overalls, underwear and socks, a face mask, and an approved crash helmet. He *should* wear driving shoes or, in an openwheeler racing car, special shoes, again preferably fire-proofed. Driving gloves are also advisable. The significance of each of these items is obvious. In recent years drivers everywhere have become much more safety-conscious in their outlook, and safety regulations and standards have improved. The fire hazard has always been serious, but recently developed synthetic fibres offer greater protection from fire than was ever before available.

Incidentally, the purpose of the face mask is not so much to protect the face from external burns, although obviously it does help in this regard, but principally to protect the lungs from the searing heat of inhaled flame.

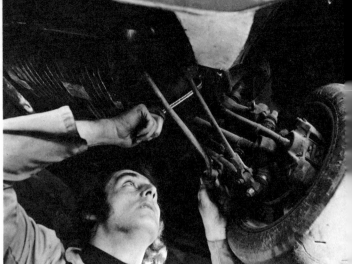

Preparing the car

In preparing a car for racing, there are again certain basic points which apply equally to a Formula One Grand Prix car or a backyard prepared lightweight touring car. Whatever stage of development you have reached, your car must handle and stop. Each significant increase in engine power will therefore call for corresponding improvement in handling and braking.

I am assuming, with the following information, that the budding race driver has an acceptable budget to work with and, for the purposes of the exercise, has elected to begin with a touring car. Fairly obviously he will have chosen a competitive car and one which suits both his budget and the class (in both size and category) appropriate to his beginner status.

He will begin by disassembling the car totally. Once it is stripped, he (and his professional mechanics if he has a large bag of gold, or his willing friends if he has a very small one) will examine each component in detail, discarding those which are to be either extensively modified or replaced with something better. Right from the outset there should be an organized plan to which the team will work. In some cases it is possible that the replacement racing components will come from the source of original manufacture; in others a great deal of creative fabrication will be necessary.

If the car is to be lightened some body panels will be replaced with fibreglass; other body components such as rear seats and interior trim will be discarded. The body will be seam welded for additional strength: that is, instead of having spot welds at regular intervals the joins will be welded all the way. It will be necessary to reinforce certain areas of considerable stress, such as suspension pick-up points. For safety reasons a roll cage will be built into the interior frame of the body. The roll cage provides protection not only from rollover but also from side and front impact. An on-board automatic fire extinguisher system should be added. Such a system can be programmed to partly fill the driving compartment with foam, activated by impact, by heat, or simply by the driver hitting a button. It is designed to allow the driver time to escape from a car which is burning or which may burn.

While the body preparation is progressing it is probable that the engine has been handed over to a development engineer whose responsibility it is to extract the best possible combination of horsepower and torque while maintaining reliability. Almost all of the original components will be changed if the adaptation is to be successful. Only the block and cylinder head will remain in any way as they were originally conceived. That is, always provided there are not limitations on the degree of engine development allowed for the chosen class of racing. We will assume he is going to do it all honestly and that the modifications are within the framework (and the spirit) of those regulations.

Back in the workshop the team will now be working on the suspension. They will be looking for a much greater degree of stiffness than was originally designed into the car and for a wider track. They will get the former with stronger springs, better quality, fully adjustable shock absorbers and equally adjustable front and rear anti-roll bars. The car will sit lower over its wheels when it is completed. The wheels themselves will probably be as wide as the regulations allow, and to accommodate them the wings will have been flared considerably.

The tyres will almost certainly not be selected until later since developments in racing tyres will take place even while the car is under construction. When they are fitted, they will be fat and squat and will have no tread pattern. There will, however, be a second set, mounted on narrower wheels perhaps, which will have drainage grooves cut into them. These will be used for racing in the rain.

By the time the car is ready to accept its shiny new high-performance engine, the gearbox and differential will have been disassembled and checked, ratios chosen, limited slip mechanism fitted, the prop shaft (if there is such a thing on this car) balanced and all will be ready for fitting.

The process of complete assembly should be slow and meticulous, with clearances and tensions checked and double-checked. Probably as a last step it will be necessary to either add or replace a number of instruments so that the driver will have all the information he needs to keep this new and expensive toy operating efficiently and (hopefully) inexpensively. Then, at long last, it's ready for track testing.

Stripping a new car right back to the metal enables a thorough examination of stress points and welds
(Photo courtesy of ABC-TV)

Track testing

This procedure in itself is almost always time-consuming and laborious. Very rarely will you hit upon the right combination of suspension settings, tune and tyre pressures right off. You will fairly quickly get down to a respectable time (always assuming your driving's not off as well), but it will take a great deal of perseverance and that 'feel' for the car we talked about earlier before you are ready to take on the world. However, if you have done everything correctly and spent your money wisely, you will probably very soon be ready to go out and do some serious motor racing.

Action

We have already mentioned that race driving is quite different from road driving. Now the time has come to qualify this remark, and to explain why.

Essentially it is because you are going so much harder. You are going deeper into corners, faster through them, and using much more of your available horsepower coming out

But in other ways it is the same as road driving. The correct line on a corner is the correct line no matter how fast you are going. It does not change (except when you change it deliberately; to defend a corner or avoid an obstacle). In race driving we talk about finesse, the delicacy of touch which distinguishes the ham-fisted amateur from the class professional. The goal in race driving, as it is in road driving, should be to be as smooth as possible at all times. If this sounds contradictory when you think about having watched a top driver in action, bear in mind that it is the sheer speed of that driver's cornering action which has made him look untidy at times. If he had not been smooth in his approach and during the corner itself, he would not have got around. The skills required to get around a corner in this manner are basically the same as those described in the earlier chapters on road driving. Eventually, however, the race driver develops a degree of sensitivity to the various movements of the car that enables him to maintain accurate control even at the much higher speeds.

Tactics

The tactics you adopt in a race will vary depending on the nature of the race and the conditions which apply at the time. The most important condition to consider is the distance of the race. A sprint race will be run differently from a long distance event. In a race of 40 miles or less the object is to go as fast as possible for the entire length of the race, but again how fast you have to drive will depend on circumstances applying within the race.

For example, if you are involved in a very close race-long dice with another driver you will have to be at maximum pressure all the way—though you still may not be as fast as you would be on the circuit on your own. If you are leading your opponent you will be forced to take slower approach lines on various corners to keep him from getting inside you under braking. If he is leading, you will be slowed by his similar tactics in trying to keep you out. On the other hand, if you are not closely pressed it will not be necessary for you to go all-out unless some driver is catching you after a pit stop or a spin. You would be better off slowing by as much as a second or so per lap, which will conserve you and your car and improve your chances of finishing. Jack Brabham has often been quoted as saying that the best way to win is as slowly as possible, and his success in long distance races confirms this approach. The only time you will be required to go as hard as possible is after an incident which has perhaps left you trailing the field.

In races of over 60 miles this rule applies even more. You will probably find that your average lap times will be as much as two or three seconds slower than your potential. In this type of race you will be relying on an efficient pit crew to keep you informed of your position in the race and your average lap times. They will be in a position to tell you whether you should go faster and a good long distance driver will rely implicitly on his pit crew's signals.

But long distance racing is a lot more complex than this. If we assume that your car is properly prepared for such racing (that is, that it will last the distance) there is a great deal of planning to be done before the flag falls.

You may need to select a co-driver who is able to drive as fast as you can or near to it and at the same time has the capacity to conserve the car. You will need to plan your pit stops and to establish accurately what fuel consumption, tyre wear and brake wear you will experience.

Some of your practice time will need to be devoted entirely to establishing these points. Even then it's a bit tricky at times. For example, let's say you are doing a race of 600 miles. In your practice sessions you have established that you can go 220 miles on a tank of fuel, but that your nearside rear tyre will only go 180 miles. The fuel consumption is fine for a two-stop schedule but the tyre won't make the distance. So to give yourself a safety margin you plan to stop at 180, 360 and 540 miles. That's one more stop than you originally wanted but it seems that you have no choice. Finally you establish that the brake pads will have to be replaced at 430 miles or thereabouts, so you plan to change them at the 360 stop.

Now, on race day, it rains for the first two hours of the race. Everything is changed. Your tyre wear and pad wear will not be so great and chances are you are also using less fuel. So while you are out driving your first session, your pit crew are hurriedly recalculating (largely by informed guesswork) to adjust the pit-stop schedule. They are not prepared to take risks with fuel consumption so they signal to you that they want the first stop at 220 miles.

When you pull in, they check both tyre and pad wear and replace the nearside rear tyre just to be sure. Then the track dries and while your co-driver is in the car it's back to the calculator once more to reschedule for the new conditions.

Now the plan is for a second stop at 400 miles, when you will take on another tyre and set of pads. This leaves you with somewhere around 125 miles to go, assuming that you are not in first place and that the front runners will complete the 600 miles before you do (and thus of course the race will be over for you too). Now the calculations are on the lead cars. Just how far in front will they be at the end? Can you make it through, or will you need that last-minute pit-stop just to be sure?

It's complicated and it's very exciting, and in such circumstances the race will be won or lost not only on the performance of you and your co-driver, nor on the performance of the car. The men who run your pit can make or break your attempt. They are vital to the cause and if you are successful in any way it will be due as much to their efforts as to any other factor.

If you've now decided to give it a go—good luck. I still think it's the most fabulous sport in the world.

The Future

14

THE FUTURE

Throughout the world, the seventies were a time of stress for the motor industry. A combination of factors all occurring at much the same time have made things exceedingly difficult for the car makers and, indirectly, for the car owner as well. In many instances the car makers have only themselves to blame for their difficulties. The American manufacturers particularly have been too short-sighted with their development programs so that when a foreseeable crisis arose they were unprepared for it.

In any practical assessment of the potential future of the auto industry, and particularly of the way in which that future will affect the consumer, it's probably desirable first to take a look at the past. Even then what any commentator says about the future is guesswork. Informed, maybe, but guesswork nevertheless.

The motor car only really became a viable commercial proposition in the first decade of this century. At that time there was a fantastic degree of excitement about the possibility of owning one of the new horseless carriages, and the minute the early scepticism was overcome, everyone wanted to climb aboard. Most motor cars were virtually handmade, and in fact well made, but the extensive amount of experimental design made them cranky and unreliable. Since the consumer knew this when he made his purchase, however, he expected nothing more. He knew that his range of travel was limited, uncomfortable and relatively expensive and he was prepared to accept such disadvantages stoically in order to become one of the pioneers.

It did not take long for things to improve. Many of the successful design concepts were adopted by all makers and even so early in the development of the automobile there arose a sameness about the range of different cars. By the mid-twenties, experimentation had very largely ceased altogether and almost all subsequent changes were developmental. They are to this day.

The standard was, and still is, an internal combustion engine driving through gearbox and drive shaft to differential to rear wheels. Obviously, there have been some tangential developments, such as front wheel drive, transverse engines, a great deal more efficiency

and reliability, more effective brakes, improved handling and comfort. All are the benefits of development, regardless of the direction such development took.

But in concept and interpretation, the car of today is not very different from the car of the twenties. Why so? Well for one thing it has been expedient for the car makers to maintain the *status quo*. As the car developed, so too, naturally enough, did the manufacturers. Many fell by the wayside for a variety of reasons (ranging from over-specialization to poor economic management). Others were absorbed by the more successful makers and as that happened so the giants grew. With the giants the possibility and hope for new concepts and a return to experimentation faded. Money was the driving force behind the automobile. As World War II faded into recent memory and societies became more affluent, the new car rapidly became the yardstick of economic status.

The auto giants fed on the 'keeping up with the Joneses' syndrome. No longer was it necessary to build anything new into a car at all. All it had to do was look different and be heavily advertised and promoted and it would sell. This was true around the world but it was more true in the United States where competition between General Motors, Ford and Chrysler particularly, became a kind of madness—a matter of who could make the least costly design changes and still create a freshly desirable car.

In Europe things were not quite so bad. At the end of the war, as Europe stabilized, there was not so much money around and the European makers concentrated their efforts on smaller cars, which were economical to run and maintain. Economical maintenance is a product of better engineering, among other things, and since Europeans kept their cars longer, the makers built in a higher degree of quality. As well, the European worker was not yet more interested in money than he was in the job and he maintained a certain pride of achievement in the cars he built. Further yet, the European had always been closer to motor racing than the American. All the pre-war and all but one of the post-war world racing champions were European or British. Hence the European revered such qualities as precise steering, accurate handling, manual gears and good brakes.

About this time the Japanese started to get in on the act. With their now legendary vigour, flexibility and enthusiasm, they first made cars which were unashamed copies of British and European counterparts. They started making for the home market but it was only a brief time before they were chasing export markets. Soon after, they stopped copying and began to be original. While they also maintained the accepted concept, they specialized in small to medium saloons and made spectacular inroads into countries where the local manufacturers were concentrating on bigger cars, the United States and Australia being prime examples.

By the mid-sixties the first bombshell burst on the American scene. The developing furore over industrial pollution caused the government to introduce pollution control laws, many of which affected the motor car. The industry in America was now to be forced to take action to reduce the harmful emission output of their automobiles, which had reached truly alarming proportions, largely due to the 'power race' which saw American engines increase in size and performance almost annually. Overnight the power race stopped and within months the American designers realized what they had known all along—that smaller engines would produce less pollutants. For a while they persevered with existing engines, however, spending literally millions of dollars on methods of emission control, and giving themselves time to introduce their 'compacts' slowly and progressively over a period of years. Less reduction in profit, you see!

Then the second bombshell. The world suddenly realized that we were running short of oil—and thus fuel. Producing countries heightened the crisis for a period by withholding their crude oil and then by substantially increasing its price. This time the whole world was affected, although once again the United States more so than most, if only because of their rate of consumption.

Almost immediately the world's motor car buyers began to ask for smaller, more economical cars. Europe could supply and Japan could supply, and countries which had previously been big car orientated became additional lucrative markets. The American manufacturers were badly affected, not just on the home market but also through their subsidiaries in Australia and South Africa where American-style cars were popular.

So the combined problems of pollution and the high cost of oil, coupled in the early seventies with world wide rampant inflation which escalated the cost of big cars beyond the reach of many, began a revolution and one for which no car maker was totally prepared.

People everywhere began to ask questions. Where were the alternatives to the petrol consuming monsters? Had the world's car makers not foreseen such a possibility? Can't we get cars which use electricity or steam instead of petrol? And the manufacturers came back, 'We have been experimenting with alternatives to the internal combustion engine for years but have not yet found a satisfactory replacement.' How convenient. At a time when science and industry can take us to the moon and beyond, can computerize and automate almost every manufacturing process known to man, can produce synthetic materials which far outperform anything known in nature, to name just a few, the auto makers would have us believe they have nothing to offer but a rehashed 1920s car.

I don't believe it and I don't think any thinking person could. The point is—how long will we, the hundreds of millions of consumers around the world, go on buying what the car makers would have us believe is the best they can do? In my opinion for not more than about another ten years!

The transition has already begun in fact. Slowly but surely the world will turn to smaller cars and in so doing they will demand the same degree of comfort they have become used to in the big cars. As well as economy and comfort they will insist upon greater ease of operation and maintenance, higher safety standards, and more effective mobility.

In the long run, beyond twenty years probably, all this will mean a total change in the concept of the car as we know it. I think (sadly, for some of us) that the job of driving will be taken away from us completely.

I foresee computerized operation of a nuclear-powered vehicle, perhaps laser or radar controlled as to route and destination, probably without wheels. I imagine we will continue with private ownership because I don't think we will ever want to lose that degree of individuality. But I think it will simply be a matter of climbing aboard your new 'car', together with wife and family, and pressing a button (or buttons) which will select the destination. The vehicle will move into the radar controlled traffic flow, home-in on a series of lasers and set off on the journey.

Probably you will be able to produce a print-out of anticipated time of arrival at any point along the way and you will have the capacity to re-programme en route for a refreshment stop, should you feel so inclined. Otherwise you may sit back and read, or sleep, or talk, or whatever.

It all sounds a bit dull really, when we compare it to our current system. But I've no doubt it will be infinitely safer and more efficient. In the meantime we still have to reach the 1990s.

While we're waiting, I think there is the distinct possibility that many car manufacturing plants will come under the control of governments and that we will see a reduction in the number of both makes and models. It is highly likely that we will see plants devoted to engine manufacture; others to transmissions; others to bodies; and yet others to final assembly. If you need a ridiculous example—a Ford engine, with Chrysler transmission in a General Motors body.

This does not necessarily mean there will not be a satisfactory choice of cars. If we had ten named manufacturers around the world, each making a range of ten models, we would still have a hundred cars to choose from. If those were all good cars (by my definition of 'good'—safe, reliable, comfortable, economical, with good handling, braking and engine performance for their size and weight) then I can't see that we would have much to complain about.

For the time being we will still also have to drive them. I said before that I am also sure that things will get worse before they get better in this regard, and I mean with relation to the rate at which people are killed or injured in cars.

Until we get universal acceptance and use of seat belts, an improved (and standardized) format for driver training, and acceptance of the fact that people are almost always responsible for their own deaths and injuries in cars, we'll go on much as we are. Even for the relatively few who really do try to do it right, there is great danger from those who don't.

In the long run what I'll miss most is the joy and the excitement of driving. Even before we are relegated to our computerized bubble cars, the roads will be so choked, the legislations so harsh, that the unique thrill of a turn at the wheel of a really good car, from any year, will be lost to us.

Make the most of it while you can.